Table of Contents

Adding Suffixes

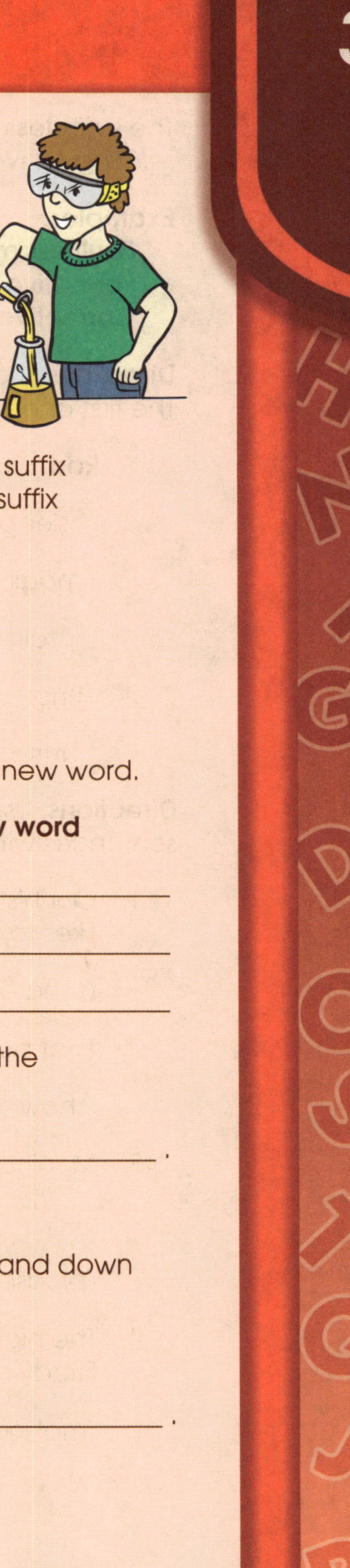

A **suffix** is a syllable at the end of a word that changes its meaning. The suffixes **ant** and **ent** mean *a person or thing that does something.*

Examples:

A person who occupies a place is an **occupant**.
A person who obeys is **obedient**.

A **root word** is the common stem that gives related words their basic meanings.

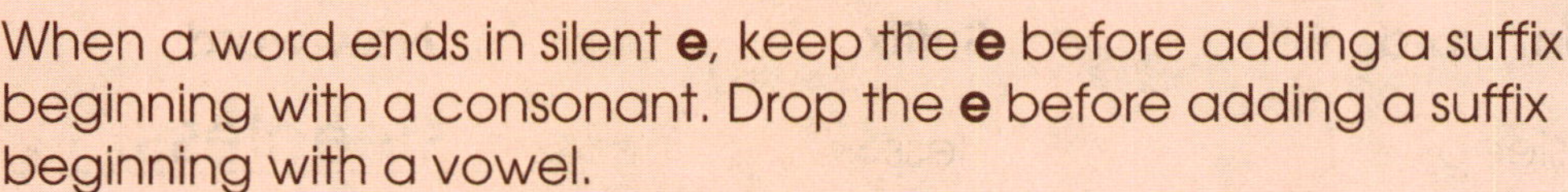

When a word ends in silent **e**, keep the **e** before adding a suffix beginning with a consonant. Drop the **e** before adding a suffix beginning with a vowel.

Examples:

announce + ment = **announcement**
announce + ing = **announcing**

Announce is the root word in this example.

Directions: Combine each root word and suffix to make a new word.

Root word	Suffix	New word
observe	ant	________________
contest	ant	________________
preside	ent	________________

Directions: Use the meanings in parentheses to complete the sentences with one of the new words above.

1. To be a good scientist, you must be very ________________ .

   (pay careful attention)

2. The game show ________________ jumped up and down when she won the grand prize.

   (person who competes)

3. Next week, we will elect a new student council ______________ .

   (highest officer)

Adding Suffixes

The suffix **less** means *without*; **ative** means *having the nature of or relating to*; **ive** means *having or tending to be.*

Examples:

Faultless means *without fault or blame.*
Formative means *something that can be formed or molded.*
Corrective means *something that fixes a problem.*

Directions: Combine each root word and suffix to form a new word. The first one is done for you.

Root word	Suffix	New word
sleep	less	sleepless
imagine	ative	____________
talk	ative	____________
impress	ive	____________
attract	ive	____________

Directions: Use the meanings in parentheses to complete the sentences with one of the new words above.

1. Our history teacher is a rather ____________________ man who likes to tell jokes and stories.

   (fond of speaking)

2. That book has such an ____________________ plot!

   (showing creativity)

3. Monica thought the dress in the store window was

   very ____________________ .

   (pleasing)

4. The high school basketball team was ____________________ in its Friday night game, beating their rivals by 30 points.

   (making an impact on the mind or emotions)

Adding Prefixes

A **prefix** is a syllable at the beginning of a word that changes its meaning. The prefixes **il**, **im**, **in**, and **ir** all mean *not*.

Examples:

Illogical means *not logical or practical.*
Impossible means *not possible.*
Invisible means *not visible.*
Irrelevant means *not relevant or practical.*

Directions: Divide each word into its prefix and root word. The first one is done for you.

	Prefix	Root Word
illogical	il	logical
impatient	______	______
immature	______	______
incomplete	______	______
insincere	______	______
irresponsible	______	______
irregular	______	______

Directions: Use the meanings in parentheses to complete the sentences with one of the words above.

1. I had to turn in my assignment ______________ because I was sick last night.
   (not finished)
2. Sue and Joel were ______________ to leave their bikes out in the rain.
   (not doing the right thing)
3. I sometimes get ______________ waiting for my ride to school.
   (restless)
4. The boys sounded ______________ when they said they were sorry.
   (not honest)
5. These towels didn't cost much because they are __________.
   (not straight or even)

Adding Prefixes

The prefix **pre** means *before*. The prefix **re** means *again*.

Examples:

Preview means *to see in advance*.
Redo means *to do again*.

Directions: Write sentences using these words with prefixes.

1. prefix ____

____

2. redirect ____

____

3. regain ____

____

4. predetermine ____

____

5. reorganize ____

____

6. prepackage ____

____

7. redistribute ____

____

Homographs

Homographs are words that have the same spelling but different meanings and pronunciations.

pres ent	n.	a gift
pre sent	v.	to introduce or offer to view
rec ord	n.	written or official evidence
re cord	v.	to keep an account of
wind	n.	air in motion
wind	v.	to tighten the spring by turning a key
wound	n.	an injury in which the skin is broken
wound	v.	past tense of wind

Directions: Write the definition for the bold word in each sentence.

1. I would like to **present** our new student council president, Mindy Hall.

   ____

2. The store made a **record** of all my payments.

   ____

3. **Wind** the music box to hear the song.

   ____

4. His **wound** was healing quickly.

   ____

5. The **wind** knocked over my bicycle.

   ____

Homophones

Homophones are words that are pronounced the same but are spelled differently and have different meanings.

Example: to, two, too

Directions: Use these homophones in sentences of your own.

1. forth ______________________________

____

2. fourth ______________________________

____

3. they're ______________________________

____

4. their ______________________________

____

5. there ______________________________

____

6. not ______________________________

____

7. knot ______________________________

____

Multiple Meanings

Directions: Circle the correct definition of the bold word in each sentence. The first one is done for you.

1. Try to **flag** down a car to get us some help!	to signal to stop cloth used as symbol
2. We listened to the **band** play the National Anthem.	group of musicians a binding or tie
3. He was the **sole** survivor of the plane crash.	bottom of the foot one and only
4. I am going to **pound** the nail with this hammer.	to hit hard a unit of weight
5. He lived on what little **game** he could find in the woods.	animals for hunting form of entertainment
6. We are going to **book** the midnight flight from Miami.	to reserve in advance a written work
7. The **pitcher** looked toward first base before throwing the ball.	baseball team member container for pouring
8. My grandfather and I played a **game** of checkers last night.	animals for hunting form of entertainment
9. They raise the **flag** over City Hall every morning.	to signal to stop cloth used as symbol

Similes

A **simile** is a comparison of two things that have something in common but are really very different. The words **like** and **as** are used in similes.

Examples:

The baby was as happy **as** a lark.
She is **like** a ray of sunshine to my tired eyes.

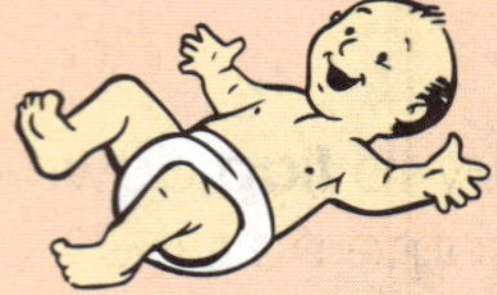

Directions: Choose a word from the box to complete each comparison. The first one is done for you.

tack	grass	fish	mule	ox	monkey

1. as stubborn as a ___mule___
2. as strong as an ________
3. swims like a ________
4. as sharp as a ________
5. climbs like a ________
6. as green as ________

Directions: Use your own words to complete these similes.

7. ________ like a bird
8. as hungry as a ________
9. as white as ________
10. as ________ as honey
11. ________ like a snake
12. as cold as ________

Directions: Use your own similes to complete these sentences.

13. Our new puppy sounded ________ .
14. The clouds were ________ .
15. The watermelon tasted ________ .

Metaphors

A **metaphor** is a direct comparison between two things. The words **like** or **as** are not used in a metaphor.

Example: The sun is a yellow ball in the sky.

Directions: Underline the metaphor in each sentence. Write the two objects being compared on the line.

1. As it bounded toward me, the dog was a quivering furball of excitement.

    ____

2. The snow we skied on was mashed potatoes.

    ____

3. John is a mountain goat when it comes to rock climbing.

    ____

4. The light is a beacon shining into the dark basement.

    ____

5. The famished child was a wolf, eating for the first time in days.

    ____

6. The man's arm was a tireless lever as he fought to win the wrestling contest.

    ____

7. The flowers were colorful circles against the green of the yard.

    ____

Idioms

An **idiom** is a phrase that says one thing but actually means something quite different.

Example: A **horse of a different color** means something quite unusual.

Directions: Write the letter of the correct meaning for each bold phrase. The first one is done for you.

a. refusal to see or listen
b. misbehaving, acting in a wild way
c. made a thoughtless remark
d. lost an opportunity
e. got angry
f. pay for
g. unknowing
h. feeling very sad
i. get married
j. excited and happy

__f__ 1. My parents will **foot the bill** for my birthday party.

_____ 2. Tony and Lisa will finally **tie the knot** in June.

_____ 3. Sam was **down in the dumps** after he wrecked his bicycle.

_____ 4. Sarah **put her foot in her mouth** when she was talking to our teacher.

_____ 5. I really **missed the boat** when I turned down the chance to work after school.

_____ 6. I got the **brush-off** from Susan when I tried to ask her where she was last night.

_____ 7. Mickey is **in the dark** about our plans to throw a surprise birthday party for him.

_____ 8. The children were **bouncing off the walls** when the baby-sitter tried to put them to bed.

_____ 9. The students were **flying high** on the last day of school.

_____ 10. My sister **lost her cool** when she discovered I had spilled chocolate milk on her new sweater.

Following Directions

Directions: Read and follow the directions.

1. Draw a vertical line from the top mid-point of the square to the bottom mid-point of the square.
2. Draw a diagonal line from top left to bottom right of the square.
3. Draw a picture of a cat's face below the square.
4. Draw a horizontal line from the left mid-point to the right mid-point of the square.
5. Draw two intersecting lines in each of the two smaller squares so they are equally divided into four quadrants.
6. Draw a triangle-shaped roof on the square.
7. Write your name in the roof section of your drawing.

Sequencing

Sequencing means *to place events in order from beginning to end or first to last.*

Example:

To send a letter, you must:
Get paper, pencil or pen, an envelope, and a stamp.
Write the letter.
Fold the letter and put it in the envelope.
Address the envelope correctly.
Put a stamp on the envelope.
Put the envelope in the mailbox or take it to the Post Office.

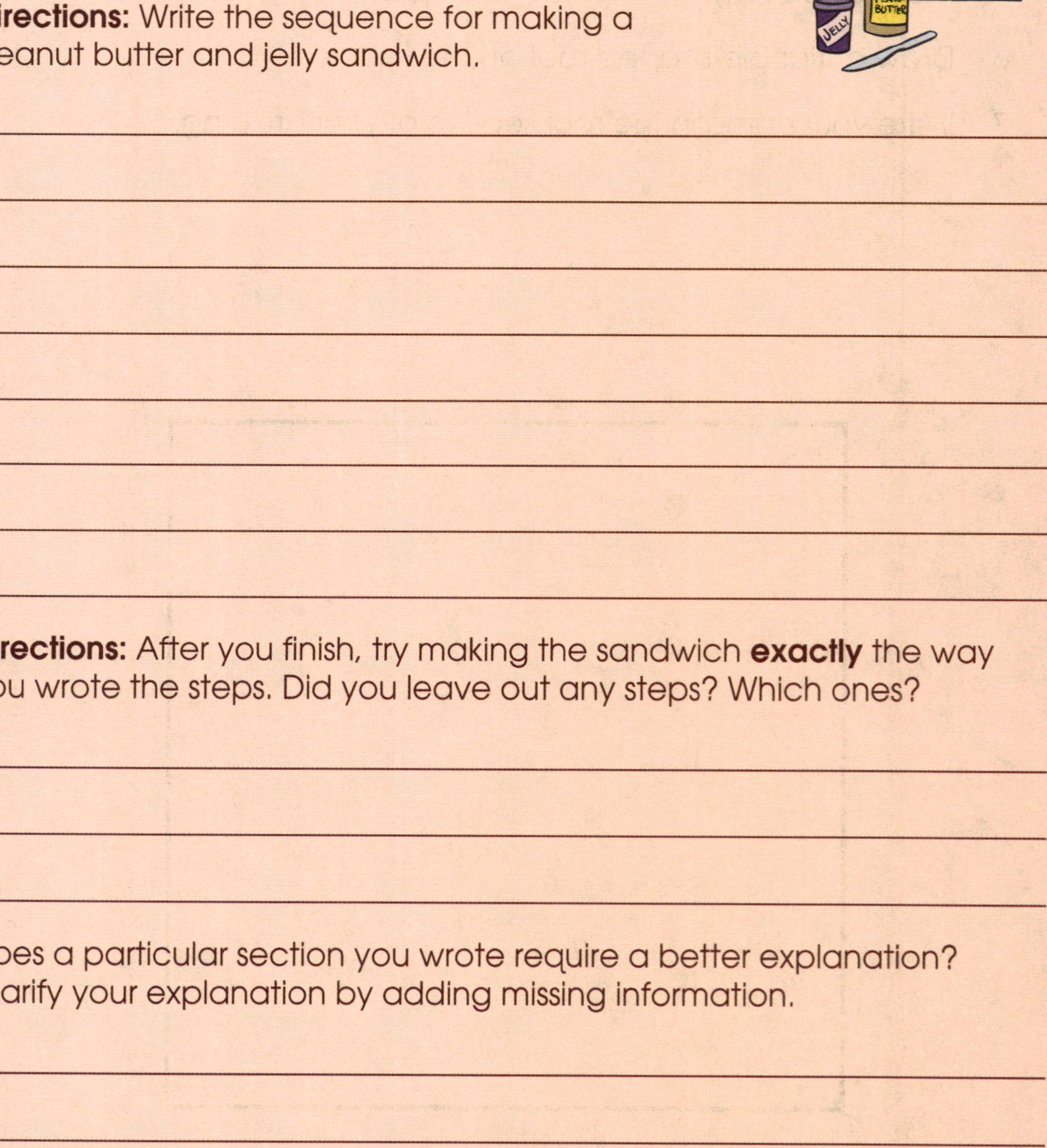

Directions: Write the sequence for making a peanut butter and jelly sandwich.

____

____

____

____

____

____

____

____

Directions: After you finish, try making the sandwich **exactly** the way you wrote the steps. Did you leave out any steps? Which ones?

____

____

____

Does a particular section you wrote require a better explanation? Clarify your explanation by adding missing information.

____

____

____

Terms and Homophones

Directions: Circle the hidden terms and homophones in the puzzle. Look up, down, backward, forward, and diagonally.

prefix	idiom	homophone	simile
suffix	homograph	metaphor	forth
fourth	shone	there	shown

Review

Directions: Circle the word or phrase that best defines the bold words.

1. The woman has a very **pleasant** voice.

   loud nice strange

2. He had a very **imaginative** excuse for not turning in his homework.

   creative difficult to believe acceptable

3. I didn't get credit for my answer on the test because it was **incomplete**.

   not correct too short not finished

4. To enroll in the school, you must bring your birth certificate or some other legal **record** for identification.

   to keep an account a flat disk that plays music

   written or official evidence

5. We use the crystal **pitcher** when we have company.

   printed likeness of a person or object

   baseball team member container for pouring

6. This block is as **light as a feather**!

   very heavy not heavy at all bright

7. The whole family was there when Bill and Lynn **tied the knot** last weekend.

   were caught in a trap bought a house

   got married

8. I will have to **foot the bill** for the damage you caused.

   kick pay for seek payment

9. Carol **lost her cool** when the party was called off.

   got angry had a fever went home

10. The kite **soared like an eagle**.

    flapped and fluttered glided along high in the air

    crashed to the ground

Review

Directions: Write the definition of each word.

1. practical ______________________________

2. attractive ______________________________

3. produce ______________________________

4. incomplete ______________________________

Directions: Write the definition of each homograph.

5. The **desert** stretched for miles with nothing but sand for a landscape.

____

6. The man felt he had no choice but to **desert** his homestead.

____

Directions: Write **S** on the line if the sentence contains a simile. Write **M** if it contains a metaphor.

7. ______ The desert was a vast ocean of sand.

8. ______ He worked as quick as lightning.

9. ______ My hand burned like fire.

Directions: Write the meaning of these idioms.

10. take the bull by the horns

____

11. bundle of nerves

____

12. at the end of your rope

____

Following Directions: Continents

Directions: Read the facts about the seven continents and follow the directions.

1. Asia is the largest continent. It has the largest land mass and the largest population. Draw a star on Asia.
2. Africa is the second largest continent. Write a **2** on Africa.
3. Australia is the smallest continent in area: three million square miles, compared to 17 million square miles for Asia. Write **3,000,000** on Australia.
4. Australia and Antarctica are the only continents entirely separated by water. Draw circles around Australia and Antarctica.
5. North America and South America are joined together by a narrow strip of land. It is called Central America. Write an **N** on North America, an **S** on South America, and a **C** on Central America.
6. Asia and Europe are joined together over such a great distance that they are sometimes called one continent. The name given to it is Eurasia. Draw lines under the names of the two continents in Eurasia.

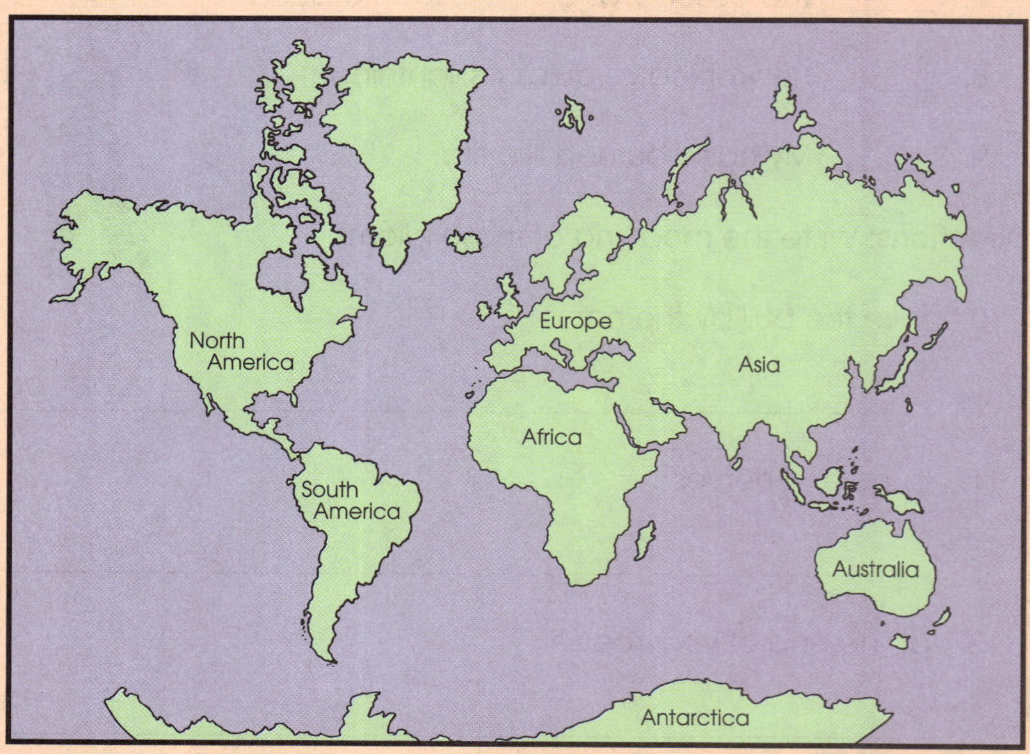

Crossword Puzzles: The World

Directions: Complete the crossword puzzle using words from the box.

Australia
Asia
Europe
Africa
Central
Eurasia
Antarctica
North

Across:

1. North America and South America are separated by a strip of land called ______________ America.
3. ______________ is entirely separated by water.
5. Italy is located on the continent of ______________ .
6. Because Europe and Asia form one large land mass, they are often referred to as ______________ .
8. ______________ is the second largest continent.

Down:

2. The United States is located on the continent of ______________ America.
4. The smallest continent in size is ______________ .
7. The largest continent is ______________ .

Finding Details: State Names

Directions: The name of a state from the box is hidden in each of the sentences below. Underline it and draw an **X** on the state in the map. The first one is done for you.

Mississippi	Connecticut	Maryland
Washington	Ohio	Vermont
Missouri	Maine	Delaware

1. I'll be at the airport when Rose Mary lands the plane for the first time.
2. While her boss is talking, the shy miss is sipping her coffee and listening politely.
3. If the cream is sour, I can't serve it to our guests.
4. After you fold it, take the washing to Nancy's house.
5. Because I wanted the phone line to disconnect, I cut the wire under the porch.
6. It is sometimes said that when you capture a fortress or citadel, a war ends.
7. Meet me after the game at the main entrance to the school.
8. Whenever Monte comes to visit, we have spaghetti for dinner.
9. "Oh, I opened the wrong door!" she said shyly.

Sequencing: Maps

Directions: Read the information about planning a map.

Maps have certain features that help you to read them. A **compass rose** points out directions. Color is often used so you can easily see where one area (such as a county, state, or country) stops and the next starts.

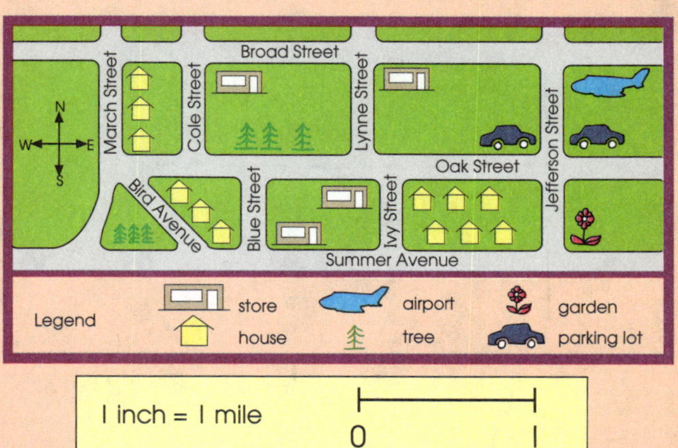

To be accurate, a map must be drawn to scale. The **scale** of a map shows how much area is represented by a given measurement. The scale can be small: one inch = one mile; or large: one inch = 1,000 miles.

Symbols are another map tool. An airplane may represent an airport. Sometimes, a symbol does not look like what it represents. Cities are often represented by dots. A map **legend** tells what each symbol means.

One of the best ways to learn about maps is to make one of your own. You may be surprised at how much you learn about your neighborhood, too. You will need a large piece of paper, a ruler, a pencil, and colored pencils.

You will need to choose the area you want to map out. It is important to decide on the scale for your map. It could be small: one inch = three feet, if you are mapping out your own backyard. Be sure to include symbols, like a picnic table to represent a park or a flag to represent a school. Don't forget to include the symbols and other important information in your legend.

Directions: Number in order the steps to making your own map.

______ Figure out the scale that will work best for your map.

______ Obtain a large piece of paper, ruler, pencil, and colored pencils.

______ Make a legend explaining the symbols you used.

______ Draw your map!

______ Draw symbols to represent features of the area you are mapping.

______ Decide on the area you want to map out.

Reading Skills: Maps

Directions: Use this map to answer the questions.

1. What state borders Louisiana to the north?

____

2. What is the state capital of Louisiana?

____

3. In which direction would you be traveling if you drove from Monroe to Alexandria?

____

4. About how far is it from Alexandria to Lake Charles?

____

5. Besides Arkansas, name one other state that borders Louisiana.

____

Reading Skills: Maps

Directions: Use this map of Columbus, Ohio, to answer the questions.

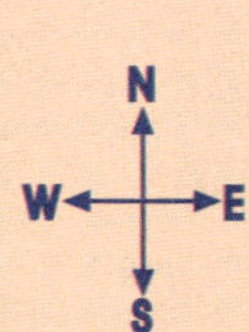

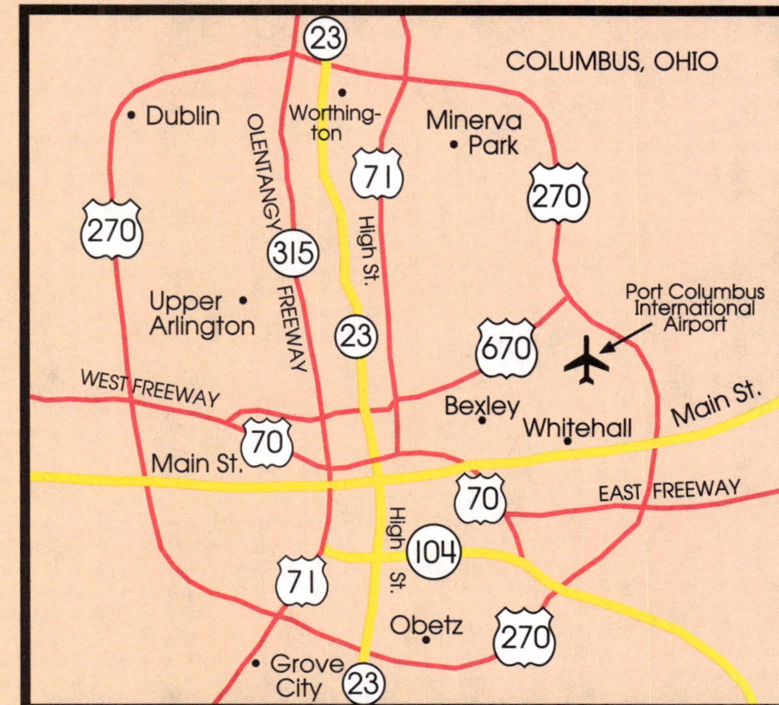

1. Does Highway 104 run east and west or north and south?

____

2. What is the name of the freeway numbered 315?

____

3. Which is farther south, Bexley or Whitehall?

____

4. Which two freeways join near the Port Columbus International Airport?

____

5. Which two suburbs are farther apart, Dublin and Upper Arlington or Dublin and Worthington?

____

Creating a Map

Directions: In the space below, draw a map of your street or town. Be sure to include a compass rose, scale, symbols, and a map legend.

Review

1. Name the seven continents.

2. On which continent is the country of China located?

3. On which continent is the country of Mexico located?

4. On which continent do you live?

5. In which state do you live?

6. What is the purpose of a map key or legend?

7. What is a compass rose?

8. The art of making maps is called *cartography*. What would a person who makes maps for a living be called?

Review

Directions: Define these words.

1. continent ______________________________

2. map ______________________________

3. cartography ______________________________

4. map legend ______________________________

5. compass rose ______________________________

Directions: Refer to the Florida map to answer the questions.

6. Florida is bordered by two bodies of water. They are:

   ____________________ and ____________________ .

7. Which National Park is located at the southernmost tip of Florida?

   ____

8. What is the state capital of Florida?

   ____

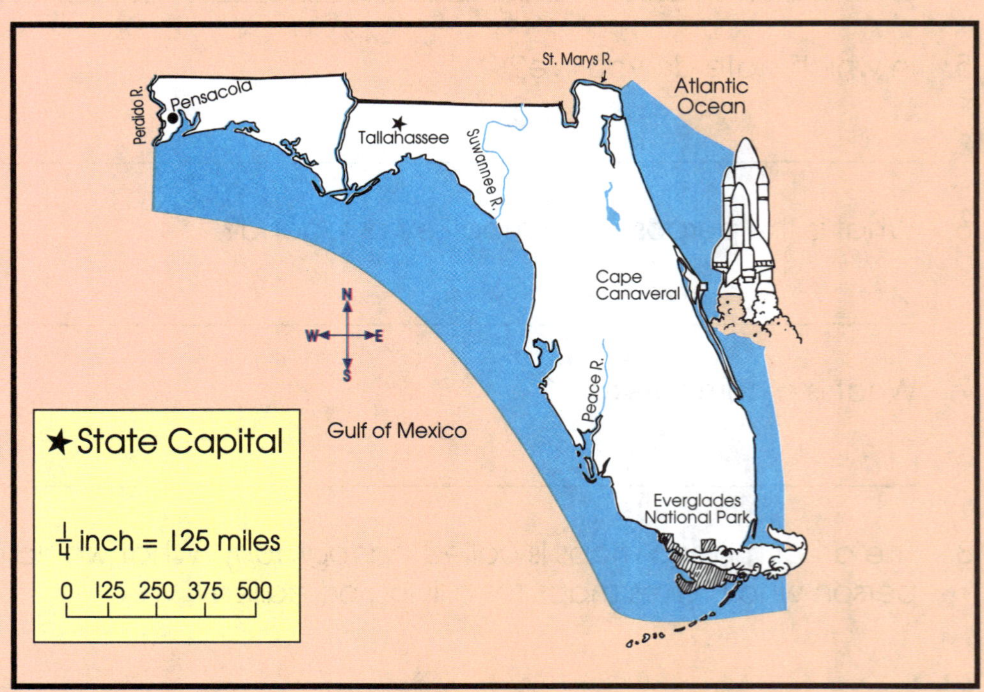

Sequencing: Winter Sleep

Directions: Read the information about hibernation.

In many areas of the world, cold winter weather can make survival difficult for living things. Plants and animals must find ways to survive the cold temperatures and lack of food and water. Plants and trees drop their leaves and rest. Many birds, some insects, and a few other animals migrate during the winter by traveling to warmer areas.

Some animals **hibernate**. Hibernation is sometimes known as "winter sleep." Mammals that hibernate include woodchucks (which are also called groundhogs), some kinds of squirrels, bats, and, of course, bears. To prepare for the winter months, these animals store up fat in their bodies during the summer and fall by eating a great amount of food. They may also hide food or take it into their dens or burrows. Some animals line their winter homes with grass or hay.

When the temperatures drop, the animals crawl into their dens. The small area helps to hold in the heat of their bodies. They fall into a deep sleep in which their bodies become almost lifeless. A hibernating bear may rouse itself occasionally and even wander about looking for a new resting place before settling into another deep sleep. The animals use up the stored fat little by little. When they wake in the spring with the warmer weather, they are thin—and ready for a big meal!

Directions: Number in order the steps a hibernating animal takes to escape winter.

______ They fall into a deep sleep in which their bodies become almost lifeless.

______ These animals store up fat in their bodies during the summer and fall.

______ When the temperatures drop, they crawl into their dens. The close space helps to hold in the heat of their bodies.

______ When they wake in the spring with the warmer weather, they are thin—and ready for a big meal!

______ The animals use up the stored fat little by little.

______ Some animals hide food or take it into their dens or burrows. They may line their winter homes with grass or hay.

Main Idea: Active Winter Animals

The **main idea** is the most important point in an article.

Directions: Read the information about animals that are active in winter. Then, answer the questions.

Although many animals hibernate during the cold winter months, there are many animals that stay active. Animals like deer, rabbits, mice, and foxes all remain in their **territory** and hunt during the winter.

These animals must eat a great deal before winter arrives in order to put on an extra layer of fat. This layer of fat is necessary to prevent them from starving when food becomes scarce in the cold weather.

Animals that stay active in the winter also grow thick coats of fur. The heavier coats act as **insulation** against the winds and cold weather and help keep them warm.

Even animals that remain active in winter need warm shelters for protection during winter storms and for sleeping. The shelters may be small holes, blankets of leaves or other **vegetation**, or rock cavities.

Winter is not an easy time for animals, but those with thick coats of fur, sufficient food, a good layer of fat, and warm shelter usually manage to survive.

1. What is the main idea of the selection?

    ____

    ____

2. What is necessary for survival in the winter?

    ____

3. Define these words. Use a dictionary if needed.

    territory ______________________________

    insulation ______________________________

    vegetation ______________________________

4. If you were an animal, would you want to hibernate or stay active? Why?

    ____

    ____

Context Clues: Migration

Using **context clues** is a way to figure out the meaning of a new word by relating it to the other words in the sentence. This is called learning the meaning from **context**.

Directions: Read the information about migration. Then, write the answers.

For hundreds of years, people believed that the yearly disappearance of some types of birds meant that they hibernated like bears and woodchucks. Today, scientists know that birds **migrate** to warmer climates for the cold winter months.

Even though scientists know that birds migrate, they are still unsure about why and how they migrate. Many birds have two homes—one for winter and one for summer. Every year, these birds travel from one place to the other. North American birds, which depend on fruit, nectar, and insects, travel south for the winter. **Tropical** birds travel north when it is too hot and dry in that area.

Migration is an amazing feat, even though it is difficult to understand and believe. Some birds travel up to 5,000 miles, and many will return to the same yard, pond, or tree each year! Birds are excellent **navigators**, and scientists believe they may use a combination of landmarks, the stars, the sun, and their hearing to help locate their destinations.

Birds also seem to know instinctively when to begin their migration. Some scientists believe that the **instinct** to migrate is aided by chemical changes in the birds' bodies brought about by shorter daylight hours.

Regardless of how or why birds migrate, the simple fact that such small animals can travel thousands of miles to the same speck of land or water is an incredible accomplishment!

1. Define these words as they are used in the article on migration.

   instinct ______________________________

   tropical ______________________________

   navigator ______________________________

2. Explain how birds find their homes while migrating.

   ____

3. Birds are born with the instinct to migrate. Name another animal that is born with an instinct and describe it.

   ____

Sequencing: Bird Feeders

Directions: Read the information about making a bird feeder.

Bird watching can be fun and educational. By providing for their basic needs—food, water, shelter, and a place to nest—you can attract birds to your own yard. Here are step-by-step instructions for making a simple bird feeder.

You will need these materials: a large can (a two-pound coffee can is a good size), a wire coat hanger, a cork, a six-inch aluminum foil pan, a nine-inch aluminum foil pan, and birdseed.

First, using the kind of can opener that cuts small triangles, make five holes in the side of the can right above the bottom rim, spacing them out evenly. Next, straighten the coat hanger and bend one end over about three inches so it forms a right angle. Poke holes the size of the coat hanger in the middle of the two foil pans. Cut another hole in the center of the bottom of the can. (Ask an adult to help you do this.) Try to make all the holes in the exact center so they will line up.

With the larger foil pan right side up, push the straight end of the coat hanger up through the hole in the pan and then through the hole in the can. Then, fill the can with birdseed, making sure the seed falls through the holes into the pan. Next, turn the smaller pan upside down and push the coat hanger through its holes to make a "lid" for the can. Then, force the cork down the coat hanger until it rests tightly against the top of the small pan, holding it in place. Finally, make a loop in the top of the coat hanger. Hang your feeder where you can easily see it. Sit back and watch the birds!

Directions: Number in order the steps to building the bird feeder.

_____ Poke holes the size of the coat hanger in the middle of the foil pans and the can.

_____ Fill the can with birdseed and make sure it falls through the holes in the sides of the can onto the bottom pan.

_____ With a can opener, make five openings in the side of the can near the bottom rim.

_____ Make a loop at the top of the coat hanger.

_____ Obtain a large can, two foil pans, a wire coat hanger, and a cork.

_____ Straighten the coat hanger and make a three-inch bend in one end.

_____ With the larger pan turned right side up, push the coat hanger up through the holes in the pan and the can.

_____ Hang up your bird feeder and watch the birds come!

_____ Turn the smaller pan upside down and push the coat hanger through its holes.

_____ Force the cork down the coat hanger until it fits tightly against the top plate.

Sequencing: Feeding Birds

Directions: Read the information about feeding birds.

Can you imagine feeding birds right from your hand? Here's how you can do that!

Begin by attracting birds to your windowsill with a bird feeder like the one described on the last page. Once they become used to feeding there, you are ready to move to the next part of the plan.

Get a piece of wood about two or three feet long and a few inches wide. Put this "arm" in the sleeve of an old coat or shirt and attach an old glove to the bottom with a thumbtack. Now, put the "arm" out the window over the bird feeder. Close the window to hold it in place. Put some birdseed on the glove every day for a week or so until the birds get used to eating from it.

Next, remove the board and put your own arm and hand inside the sleeve and glove. Rest your arm on the windowsill so it doesn't get tired, and hold some birdseed in your hand. Be very still! After a few days, the birds will get used to eating from your gloved hand. The next step is to take off the glove and put the seed in your bare hand. You will have birds feeding out of your hand in no time!

Directions: Number in order the steps for getting birds to eat from your hand.

_____ Rest your arm on the windowsill and put birdseed in your gloved hand. Hold very still!

_____ Make an "arm" from a piece of wood. Put it inside the sleeve of a coat or shirt and attach an old glove to the bottom.

_____ When the birds become used to eating from your gloved hand, take off the glove.

_____ Stick the "arm" out the window over the bird feeder and put birdseed in the glove.

_____ Put birdseed in your bare hand and wait for the birds to begin eating from your hand.

_____ Start attracting birds to your windowsill with a bird feeder. Let them get used to feeding there.

_____ Once the birds are used to feeding from the "arm" you made, put your own hand and arm into the sleeve and glove.

Sequencing: Caterpillars

Directions: Read the information about caterpillars.

For a long time, people believed that the caterpillar and the butterfly were two unrelated insects. Today, however, we know that they are the same creature at different stages of development.

This remarkable life cycle begins when the female butterfly lays her eggs—which can number in the hundreds—on a plant that will provide exactly the right food for the caterpillars that will hatch. When a caterpillar hatches, it begins eating right away and continues to eat constantly. Soon it is too big for its skin. The skin splits to allow the caterpillar to crawl out. This is called molting. The caterpillar may molt as many as 10 times before beginning the next stage of development.

During the next stage, called the pupa, there seems to be little activity, but in fact, many changes are taking place inside the caterpillar. The caterpillar finds a place, usually on a twig, and deposits a sticky liquid to form a pad. This liquid acts like glue, holding the caterpillar to the twig. The caterpillar then hangs upside down. The skin molts one final time. Immediately, a hard shell called a chrysalis or cocoon forms around the caterpillar.

After 10 to 14 days, the cocoon suddenly bursts open. A few seconds later, a butterfly comes out. At first, its wings are pressed together. Fluid is pumped through hollow veins until the wings are fully expanded. The butterfly spreads its wings to dry and harden them. Then, the fluid is withdrawn from the wing veins. The butterfly is now ready to fly.

Directions: Number in order the stages of a butterfly's life cycle.

______ A few seconds later, a butterfly comes out.

______ A hard shell called a chrysalis or cocoon is formed.

______ The female butterfly lays her eggs on a plant.

______ The caterpillar's skin splits to allow it to crawl out.

______ The caterpillar eats constantly.

______ The butterfly is now ready to fly.

______ After 10 to 14 days, the cocoon suddenly bursts open.

______ The caterpillar's skin molts one final time.

______ Fluid fills the butterfly's wings, which then dry and harden.

Review

Directions: Write the answers.

1. Define hibernation. ______________________________

____

2. Name an animal that hibernates. ______________________________

3. Define migration. ______________________________

____

4. Name an animal that migrates. ______________________________

5. Do you have a bird feeder at home? ______________________________

6. Why is it important to keep the bird feeder filled with seeds throughout the winter?

____

____

7. What four stages of development does a butterfly go through?

____

____

Review

Directions: Write the answers.

1. Explain the difference between hibernation and migration.

   ____

   ____

   ____

2. List at least three animals that fit each category.

Hibernates	Migrates
____________________	____________________
____________________	____________________
____________________	____________________

3. Consider this problem: A man enjoys feeding birds in his wooded backyard during winter. However, because there are many trees, he also has a large squirrel population. Whenever he fills his bird feeders, they are emptied within minutes by the crafty and gymnastic squirrels.

   What can the man do to solve his problem? Explain your solution in paragraph form below.

   ____

   ____

   ____

   ____

   ____

   ____

Classifying

Classifying means *putting items into categories based on similar characteristics.*

Example: Apple pie, cookies, and ice cream could be classified as desserts.

Directions: Cross out the word in each group that does not belong. Then, add a word of your own that does belong. The first one is done for you.

1.	wren	robin	~~feather~~
	sparrow	eagle	bluebird
2.	sofa	stool	chair
	carpet	bench	__________
3.	lettuce	salad	corn
	broccoli	spinach	__________
4.	pencil	chalk	crayon
	pen	drawing	__________
5.	perch	shark	penguin
	bass	tuna	__________

Directions: Write a category name above each group of words. Then, write a word of your own that belongs in each group.

__________	__________
blizzard	ankle
hurricane	shin
thunder	thigh
__________	__________

__________	__________
antenna	hockey
speaker	ice skating
battery	bobsledding
__________	__________

Classifying

Directions: Write three objects which could belong in each category.

1. whales ______ ______ ______
2. songs ______ ______ ______
3. sports stars ______ ______ ______
4. fruit ______ ______ ______
5. schools ______ ______ ______
6. teachers ______ ______ ______
7. tools ______ ______ ______
8. friends ______ ______ ______
9. books ______ ______ ______
10. mammals ______ ______ ______
11. fish ______ ______ ______
12. desserts ______ ______ ______
13. cars ______ ______ ______
14. hobbies ______ ______ ______
15. vegetables ______ ______ ______

Classifying: Regional Forecast

Directions: Read the forecast. Then, write words in the correct categories.

The very warm, early spring weather will continue to spread along the East Coast today. With some sunshine, afternoon temperatures will climb to 90 degrees in many places. Columbia, South Carolina, and neighboring areas could reach 100 degrees. Showers are expected from Washington, D.C., to New York City. Severe thunderstorms are likely in Virginia and North Carolina. Central South Carolina will be under a tornado watch during the afternoon.

Cities

____

____

____

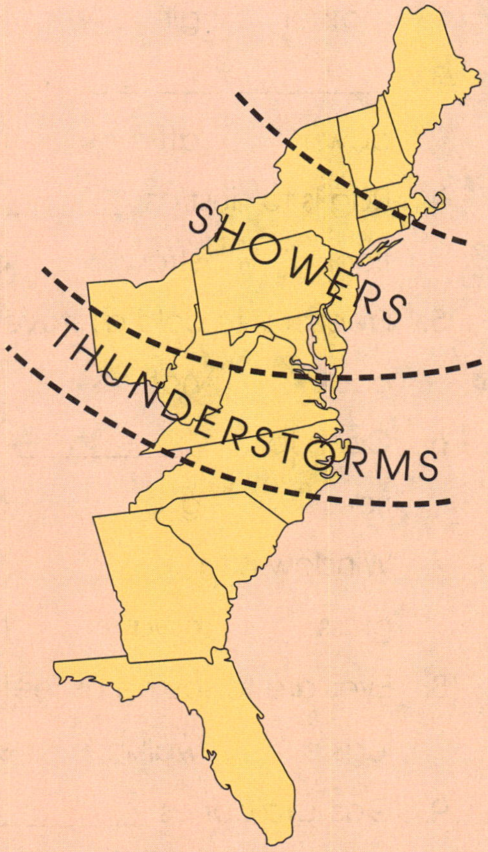

States

____

____

____

Weather Conditions

____

____

____

____

SHOWERS

THUNDERSTORMS

Analogies

An **analogy** is a way of comparing objects to show how they relate.

Example: Nose is to smell as tongue is to taste.

Directions: Write the correct word on the blank to fill in the missing part of each analogy. The first one is done for you.

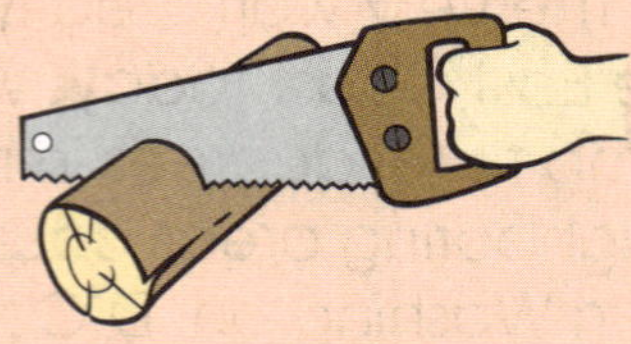

1. Scissors are to paper as saw is to wood.
   fold scissors thin
2. Man is to boy as woman is to ________________ .
   mother girl lady
3. ________________ is to cellar as sky is to ground.
   down attic up
4. Rag is to dust as ________________ is to sweep.
   floor straw broom
5. Freezer is to cold as stove is to ________________ .
   cook hot recipe
6. Car is to ________________ as book is to bookshelf.
   ride gas garage
7. Window is to ________________ as car is to metal.
   glass clear house
8. Eyes are to seeing as feet are to ________________ .
   legs walking shoes
9. Gas is to car as ________________ is to lamp.
   electricity plug cord
10. Refrigerator is to food as ________________ is to clothes.
    fold material closet
11. Floor is to down as ceiling is to ________________ .
    high over up
12. Pillow is to soft as rock is to ________________ .
    dirt hard hurt

Analogies

Directions: Write your own words on the blanks to complete each analogy. The first one is done for you.

1. Fuse is to firecracker as wick is to ____candle____.
2. Wheel is to steering as ____________ is to stopping.
3. Scissors are to ____________ as needles are to sew.
4. Water is to skiing as rink is to ____________.
5. Steam shovel is to dig as tractor is to ____________.
6. Stick is to hockey as ____________ is to baseball.
7. Watch is to television as ____________ is to radio.
8. ____________ are to goose as children are to child.
9. Multiply is to multiplication as ____________ is to subtraction.
10. Milk is to cow as egg is to ____________.
11. Yellow is to banana as ____________ is to tomato.
12. ____________ is to slow as day is to night.
13. Pine is to tree as ____________ is to flower.
14. Zipper is to jacket as ____________ is to shirt.
15. Museum is to painting as library is to ____________.

Facts and Opinions

A **fact** is information that can be proved.

Example: Hawaii is a state.

An **opinion** is a belief. It tells what someone thinks. It cannot be proved.

Example: Hawaii is the prettiest state.

Directions: Write **f** (fact) or **o** (opinion) on the line by each sentence. The first one is done for you.

__f__ 1. Hawaii is the only island state.

_____ 2. The best fishing is in Michigan.

_____ 3. It is easy to find a job in Wyoming.

_____ 4. Trenton is the capital of New Jersey.

_____ 5. Kentucky is nicknamed the Bluegrass State.

_____ 6. The friendliest people in the United States live in Georgia.

_____ 7. The cleanest beaches are in California.

_____ 8. Summers are most beautiful in Arizona.

_____ 9. Only two percent of North Dakota is forest or woodland.

_____ 10. The first shots of the Civil War were fired in South Carolina on April 12, 1861.

_____ 11. The varied geographical features of Washington include mountains, deserts, a rainforest, and a volcano.

_____ 12. In 1959, Alaska and Hawaii became the 49th and 50th states admitted to the Union.

_____ 13. Wyandotte Cave, one of the largest caves in the United States, is in Indiana.

Directions: Write one fact and one opinion about your own state.

Fact: ____

____

Opinion: ____

____

Facts and Opinions

Directions: Read the articles about cats. List the facts and opinions.

Cats make the best pets. Domestic or house cats were originally produced by crossbreeding several varieties of wild cats. They were used in ancient Egypt to catch rats and mice, which were overrunning bins of stored grain. Today, they are still the most useful domestic animal.

Facts:

____

____

____

Opinions:

____

____

It is bad luck for a black cat to cross your path. This is one of the many legends about cats. In ancient Egypt, for example, cats were considered sacred, and often were buried with their masters. During the Middle Ages, cats often were killed for taking part in what people thought were evil deeds. Certainly, cats sometimes do bring misfortune.

Facts:

____

____

____

Opinions:

____

____

Cause and Effect

A **cause** is an event or reason that has an effect on something else.

Example:

The heavy rains produced flooding in Chicago.
Heavy rains were the **cause** of the flooding in Chicago.

An **effect** is an event that results from a cause.

Example:

Flooding in Chicago was due to the heavy rains.
Flooding was the **effect** caused by the heavy rains.

Directions: Read the paragraphs. Complete the charts by writing the missing cause (reason) or effect (result).

Club-footed toads are small toads that live in the rainforests of Central and South America. Because they give off a poisonous substance on their skins, other animals cannot eat them.

Cause: They give off a poisonous substance.

Effect: ____________________

Bluebirds can be found in most areas of the United States. Like other members of the thrush family of birds, young bluebirds have speckled breasts. This makes them difficult to see and helps them hide from their enemies. The Pilgrims called them "blue robins" because they are much like the English robin. They are the same size and have the same red breast and friendly song as the English robin.

Cause: Young bluebirds have speckled breasts.

Effect: ____________________

Cause: ____________________

Effect: The Pilgrims called them "blue robins."

Review

Directions: Cross out the word that does not belong. Replace it with a word of your own.

1. oak wood maple pine ________________
2. roots stem petal dirt ________________
3. paragraph newspaper magazine book ________________

Directions: Circle the word that completes each analogy. Write it on the line.

4. Bear is to woods as fish is to ____________________ .

   sea eggs scales

5. Sit is to chair as ____________________ is to bed.

   night bedroom lie

6. ____________________ is to window as rug is to floor.

   curtain glass open

Directions: Write **f** (fact) or **o** (opinion) to describe each sentence.

_____ 7. Australia is the smallest continent.

_____ 8. The Australians are the friendliest people in the world.

_____ 9. You will see kangaroos and koalas in Australia.

Directions: Write the letter of the effect next to its cause.

	Cause	**Effect**
10.	______ As fuel supplies dwindle,	a. we had few flowers this spring.
11.	______ Because she wants to help sick people,	b. Jacob wouldn't eat his broccoli.
12.	______ It had stormed the night before,	c. Mary plans to go to medical school.
13.	______ Because he doesn't like vegetables,	d. prices will rise.
14.	______ Because the squirrels ate our tulip bulbs,	e. and many large trees were toppled.

Review

Directions: Write the answers.

1. Define classifying.

____

2. Add words to these classifications:

meat:
hamburger
steak
sirloin tip

music groups:
the Jonas Brothers
the Beatles

breakfast drinks:
orange juice
cranberry juice
grapefruit juice

colors:
blue
fuschia
melon

3. Give an example of an analogy. _______________

4. Write two sentences that are facts.

____

____

5. Write two sentences that are opinions.

____

____

6. Write an example of cause and effect. Underline the cause. Circle the effect.

____

____

Review

Directions: Write a category name for each group.

1.	blue jay	robin	chickadee	______________
2.	baseball	soccer	football	______________
3.	cumulus	cirrus	stratus	______________
4.	Orion	Cassiopeia	Big Dipper	______________
5.	humpback	blue	killer	______________

Directions: Complete these analogies.

6. Engine is to car as heart is to ______________ .
7. Yellow is to banana as red is to ______________ .
8. Photo is to camera as ______________ is to camcorder.

Directions: Write two facts and two opinions about a sport.

Facts:

9. ______________________________
10. ______________________________

Opinions:

11. ______________________________
12. ______________________________

Directions: Complete these sentences with an effect.

13. She enjoyed the book so she ______________ .
14. Because my teacher is absent, ______________ .
15. My mom likes broccoli so ______________ .

Reading Comprehension: Printing

Directions: Read the information about printing. Then, answer the questions.

When people talk about printing, they usually mean making exact copies of an original document, such as a newspaper, magazine, or an entire book. The inventions that have allowed us to do this are some of the most important developments in history. Look around you at the many examples of printed materials. Can you imagine life without them?

Until the thirteenth century, all material had to be printed by hand, one copy at a time. To make a copy of a book took much time and effort.

The oldest known example of a printed book was made in China in 848 A.D. by Wang Chieh, who carved each page of a book by hand onto a block of wood. He then put ink on the wood and pressed it on paper. The idea of printing with wood blocks spread to Europe.

In about 1440, the German goldsmith Johann Gutenberg developed the idea of **movable type**. He invented separate letters made of metal for printing. The letters could be joined together to make words and sentences. Ink was applied to the letters to print many copies of the same material. Because they were made of metal, the letters could be used over and over. This wonderful invention made it possible to have more printed material at a lower cost.

Gutenberg had other ideas that were important to printing. He developed a special type of ink that would stick to the new metal letters. Gutenberg's ideas were so successful that the process of printing went almost unchanged for more than 300 years.

1. In what country was the oldest known printed book made?

 ____

2. Who made the first printed book?

 ____

3. What is **movable type**?

 ____

4. Who developed the idea of movable type?

 ____

5. What was another important invention of Gutenberg?

 ____

Reading Comprehension: Newspapers

Directions: Read the information about newspapers. Then, answer the questions.

Newspapers keep us informed about what is going on in the world. They entertain, educate, and examine the events of the day. For millions of people worldwide, newspapers are an important part of daily life.

Newspapers are published at various intervals, but they usually come out daily or weekly. Of the nearly 60,000 newspapers published around the world, about 2,600 are published in the United States. More than half—about 1,800—of them are dailies.

Some newspapers have many **subscribers**—people who pay to have each edition delivered to them. *The Wall Street Journal* and *USA Today* each have about two million subscribers. There are many, many newspapers with only a few thousand subscribers. These include small-town weeklies and special-interest papers, like those written for people who enjoy the same hobby.

Newspapers provide a service to the community by providing information at little cost. But newspaper publishing is a business, so like other businesses, newspapers need to make money. They can keep the cost to subscribers low and still stay in business by selling space to businesses and individuals who want to advertise products or services. In most newspapers, between one-third and two-thirds of the paper is taken up by advertising.

1. About how many newspapers are published worldwide?

   ____

2. What services do newspapers provide?

   ____

3. What are **subscribers**?

   ____

4. How often are most newspapers published?

   ____

5. What do newspapers do to keep the cost to the reader low, but still make money?

   ____

6. In most newspapers, about how much of the paper is taken up by advertising?

   ____

Reading Comprehension: Newspapers

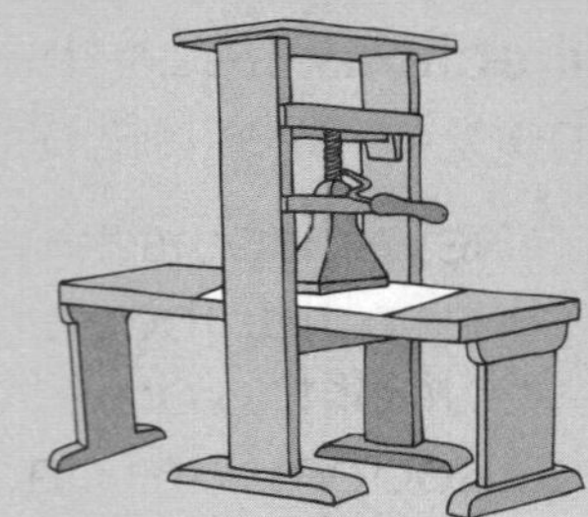

Directions: Read the information about the first newspapers. Then, answer the questions.

Long ago, town criers walked through cities reading important news to the people. The earliest newspapers were probably handwritten notices posted in towns for the public to read.

The first true newspaper was a weekly paper started in Germany in 1609. It was called *The Strassburg Relation*. The Germans were pioneers in newspaper publishing. Johann Gutenberg, the man who developed movable type, was German.

One of the first English-language newspapers, *The London Gazette*, was first printed in England in 1665. Gazette is an old English word that means *official publication*. Many newspapers today still use the word gazette in their names.

In America, several papers began during colonial days. The first successful one, *The Boston News-Letter*, began printing in 1704. It was very small—about the size of a sheet of notebook paper with printing on both sides.

An important date in newspaper publishing was 1833. In that year, *The New York Sun* became the first penny newspaper. The paper actually did cost only a penny. The penny newspapers were similar to today's papers: they printed news while it was still new, they were the first to print advertisements and to sell papers in newsstands, and they were the first to be delivered to homes.

1. How were the earliest newspapers different from today's newspapers?

   ____

2. In what year and where was the first true newspaper printed?

   ____

3. What was the name of the first successful newspaper in America?

   ____

4. List four ways penny newspapers were like the newspapers of today.

   ____

   ____

   ____

   ____

Reading Comprehension: Newspaper Jobs

Directions: Read the information about jobs at a newspaper. Then, answer the questions.

It takes an army of people to put out one of the big daily newspapers. Three separate departments are needed to make a newspaper operate smoothly: editorial, mechanical, and business.

The editorial department is the one most people think about first. That is the news-gathering part of the newspaper. The most familiar job in this department is that of the reporter—the person who obtains information for a story and writes it. A photographer takes pictures to go along with the reporter's story.

Editors are the decision-makers. There are many editors at a large newspaper. They assign stories to reporters, read the stories to be certain they are correct, and decide where and if the stories should appear in the paper. The most important stories go on the front page. There are also photo editors who choose which pictures will appear in the paper. Other workers in the editorial department include artists, copy editors, proofreaders, and cartoonists.

The biggest job in the mechanical department is printing the paper. Most large newspapers have their own printing presses. Some small papers send their work to outside printing shops. After an issue, or edition, is printed, it is ready to be sold, or circulated, to the public.

Circulation of the paper is one of the jobs of the business department. This department also sells advertising space. This is very important for newspapers. Many papers make more money selling advertising space than selling newspapers. The business department also takes care of normal business jobs, like paying employees, paying bills, and keeping records.

1. What are the three main departments at a newspaper?

   ____

2. Who gets the information for a story and writes it?

   ____

3. Who are the decision-makers at a newspaper?

   ____

4. What is the biggest job for the mechanical department?

   ____

5. What is the most important job of the business department?

   ____

Reading Comprehension: News Stories

Directions: Read the information about news stories. Then, draw a ✓ in the box to show the correct meaning of the bold word.

Here is an example of how a story gets into the newspaper:

Let's imagine that a city bus has turned over in a ditch, injuring some of the passengers. An **eyewitness** calls the newspaper. The editor assigns a reporter to go to the scene. The reporter talks to the passengers, driver, and witnesses who saw the accident. He or she finds out what they saw and how they feel, writing down their comments or tape recording their answers. At the same time, a photographer is busy taking pictures.

If there isn't time for the reporter to go back to the newsroom, reporters can use laptops to write the story on the spot.

Next, an editor reads the story, checking facts, grammar, and spelling. Meanwhile, the photographer chooses a photo.

The story is set in print. A **proofreader** checks the story for mistakes. The newspaper is now ready for printing. The presses begin to run.

Miles of paper are turned into thousands of printed, cut, and folded newspapers. They are counted, put into bundles, and placed in waiting trucks. Within a few hours, people can read about the bus accident in their daily newspaper.

1. Based on the other words in the sentence, what is the correct definition of **eyewitness**?
   - ❑ a reporter
   - ❑ a person who saw what happened
   - ❑ a lawyer
2. Based on the other words in the sentence, what is the correct definition of **proofreader**?
   - ❑ person who checks for mistakes
   - ❑ person who shows proof he has read a book
   - ❑ a teacher

Reading Comprehension: News Services

Directions: Read the information about news services. Then, answer the questions.

When people read daily newspapers, they expect to see current news from all over the world. Some newspapers have offices or reporters in Washington, D.C. and other major cities around the world. Most newspapers rely on news services for international news. News services are organizations that gather and sell news to papers, radio, and television stations. They are sometimes referred to as wire services, because they originally sent stories over telegraph or Teletype lines, or wires.

The two largest news services are the Associated Press and United Press International. Stories sent by these services have their initials—AP or UPI—at the beginning of the article. All large American newspapers are members of either the AP or UPI service.

At one time, people had to wait for messengers to arrive by foot, horse, or ship to learn the news. By the time it reached a newspaper, news could be months old.

Gathering news from around the world became much faster after the invention of the telegraph, Teletype, telephone, and transatlantic cable. Today, satellites, modems, and fax machines can send stories, pictures, and even videos around the world in seconds.

1. What is another name for news service organizations?

____

2. What are three inventions that have speeded up worldwide news-gathering?

____

3. Why do newspapers use news services?

____

4. How was news delivered before the invention of modern communication devices?

____

Reading Comprehension: Samuel Clemens

Directions: Read the information about Samuel Clemens.

Samuel Langhorne Clemens was born in Florida, Missouri, in 1835. In his lifetime, he gained worldwide fame as a writer, lecturer, and humorist.

Clemens first worked for a printer when he was only 12 years old. Soon after that, he worked on his brother's newspaper.

Clemens traveled frequently and worked as a printer in New York, Philadelphia, St. Louis, and Cincinnati. On a trip to New Orleans in 1857, he learned the difficult art of steamboat **piloting**. Clemens loved piloting and later used it as a background for some of his books, including *Life on the Mississippi*.

A few years later, Clemens went to Nevada with his brother and tried gold mining. When this proved unsuccessful, he went back to writing for newspapers. At first, he signed his humorous pieces Josh. In 1863, he began signing them Mark Twain. The words "mark twain" were used by riverboat pilots to mean *two fathoms (12 feet) deep*, water deep enough for steamboats. From then on, Clemens used this now-famous **pseudonym** for all his writing.

As Mark Twain, he received attention from readers all over the world. His best-known works include *Tom Sawyer* and *The Adventures of Huckleberry Finn*. These two books about boyhood adventures remain popular with readers of all ages.

MARK TWAIN

Directions: Check the correct answer.

1. Based on the other words in the sentence, what is the correct definition of **pseudonym**?
   - ❑ book title
   - ❑ a made-up name used by an author
   - ❑ a humorous article
2. Based on the other words in the sentence, what is the correct definition of **piloting**?
   - ❑ driving an airplane
   - ❑ steering a steamboat on a river
   - ❑ being a train engineer

Review

Directions: Write the answers.

1. What are two ways newspapers earn money?

___

___

2. What was Mark Twain's real name?

___

3. Name six jobs at a newspaper.

___

___

___

___

___

___

4. What is the purpose of the Associated Press and the United Press International?

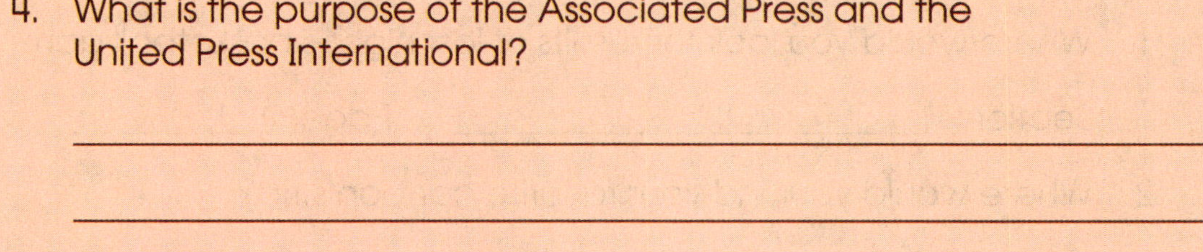

___

___

___

___

___

Reading Skills: A Newspaper Index

An **index** is a listing in a book, magazine, or newspaper that tells where to find items or information.

Newspapers provide many kinds of information. You can read about national events, local news, the weather, and sports. You will also find opinions, feature stories, advice columns, comics, entertainment, recipes, advertisements, and more. A guide that tells you where to find different types of information in a newspaper is called a *newspaper index*. An index of the newspaper usually appears on the front page.

Directions: Use the newspaper index to answer the questions.

Business 8	Local News 5–7
Classified Ads 18–19	National News 1–4
Comics 20	Radio-TV 17
Editorials 9	Sports 11–13
Entertainment 14–16	Weather 10

1. Where would you look for results of last night's basketball games?

   Section: ______________________ Page(s) __________

2. Where would you find your favorite cartoon strip?

   Section: ______________________ Page(s) __________

3. Where would you find opinions of upcoming elections?

   Section: ______________________ Page(s) __________

4. Where would you look to locate a used bicycle to buy?

   Section: ______________________ Page(s) __________

5. Where would you find out if you need to wear your raincoat tomorrow?

   Section: ______________________ Page(s) __________

6. Which would be first, a story about the president's trip to Europe or a review of the newest movie?

   ____

Reading Skills: Newspapers

Directions: Write the answers.

1. What is the name of your daily local newspaper?

 ____

2. List the sections included in your local newspaper.

 ____

3. What sections of the newspaper do you read on a regular basis?

 ____

4. Find the editorial section of your newspaper. An editorial is the opinion of one person. Write the main idea of one editorial.

 ____

 ____

 ____

5. If you could work at a newspaper, which job would you like? Why?

 ____

 ____

 ____

Directions: Read a copy of *USA Today*. You can find a copy in most libraries. Compare it to your local paper.

6. How are they alike? ______________________________

 ____

7. How are they different? ______________________________

 ____

Reading Skills: Classified Ads

A **classified ad** is an advertisement in a newspaper or magazine offering a product or service for sale or rent.

Example: For Sale: Used 26″ 30-speed bike. $100.
Call 555-5555.

Directions: Read these advertisements.
Answer the questions.

1.
Yard Work
Breaking Your Back?
Give Mike and Jane a crack! Mowing, raking, trash hauled. References provided. Call 555-9581.

2.
Pet Sitter:
Going on vacation? Away for the weekend? I am 14 years old and have experience caring for dogs and cats. Your home or mine. Excellent references. Call Sally Trent. Phone: 999-8250.

3.
Singing Lessons for All Ages!
Be popular at parties! Fulfill your dreams! 20 years coaching experience. Madame Rinaud . . . Coach to the Stars. 555-5331.

1. What is promised in the third ad? ______________________

____

2. Is it fact or opinion? ______________________

3. What fact is offered in the third ad? ______________________

____

4. Which ad gives the most facts? ______________________

5. Which ad is based mostly on opinion? ______________________

Reading Skills: Classified Ads

Directions: Write a classified ad for these topics. Include information about the item, a phone number, and an eye-catching title.

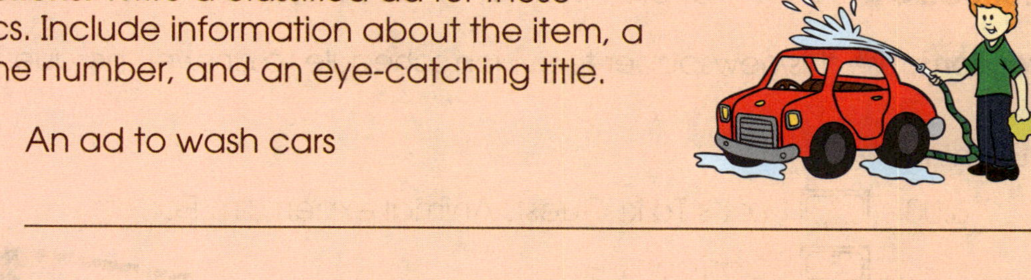

1. An ad to wash cars

____

____

____

2. An ad for free puppies

____

____

____

3. An ad for something you would like to sell

____

____

4. An ad to sell your house

____

____

____

____

____

Reading Skills: Schedules

A **schedule** lists events or programs by time, date, and place or channel.

Directions: Use this newspaper television schedule to answer the questions.

Evening

Time	Channel	Program
6:00	3	Let's Talk! Guest: Animal expert Jim Porter
	5	Cartoons
	8	News
	9	News
7:00	3	Farm Report
	5	Movie. *A Laugh a Minute* (1955) James Rayburn. Comedy about a boy who wants to join the circus.
	8	Spin for Dollars!
	9	Cooking with Cathy. Tonight: Chicken with mushrooms
7:30	3	Double Trouble (comedy). The twins disrupt the high school dance.
	8	Wall Street Today: Stock Market Report
8:00	3	NBA Basketball. Teams to be announced.
	8	News Special. "Saving Our Waterways: Pollution in the Mississippi."
	9	Movie. *At Day's End* (1981). Michael Collier, Julie Romer. Drama set in World War II.

1. What two stations have the news at 6:00? ______________________

2. What time would you turn on the television to watch a funny movie? ______________ What channel? ______________

3. What could you watch if you are a sports fan?

   ____

   What time and channel is it on? ______________________

4. Which show title sounds like it could be a game show?

   ____

Reading Skills: Labels

Labels provide information about products.

Directions: Read the label on the medicine bottle. Answer the questions.

Remember: Children should never take medicines without their parents' knowledge and consent.

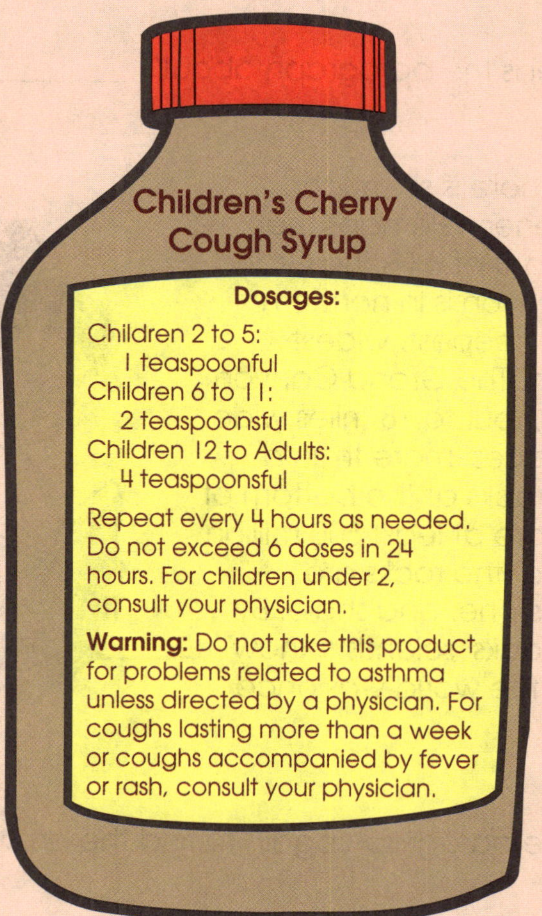

1. What is the dosage, or amount to be taken, for a 3-year-old child?

____

2. How often can you take this medicine if it is needed?

____

3. How many times a day can you take this medicine?

____

4. What should you do before taking the medicine if you have a rash in addition to your cough?

____

Reading Skills: Skimming

Skimming an article means *to read quickly, looking for headings and key words to give an overall idea of the content of an article or to find a particular fact.* When skimming for answers, read the questions first. Then, look for specific words that will help locate the answers.

Directions: Skim the paragraph to answer this question.

1. What marvel is the paragraph about? ______________________

In America, there is so much magnificent scenery. Perhaps the most stunning sight of all is the Grand Canyon. This canyon is in northern Arizona. It is the deepest, widest canyon on Earth. The Grand Canyon is 217 miles long, four to 18 miles wide and, in some places, more than a mile deep. The rocks at the bottom of the steep walls are at least 500 million years old. Most of the rocks are sandstone, limestone, and shale. By studying these rocks, scientists know that this part of the world was once under the sea.

Directions: Skim the paragraph again to find the answers to these questions.

1. How deep are the lowest points in the Grand Canyon?

____

2. How old are the rocks at the bottom of the Grand Canyon?

____

3. What kinds of rocks would you find in the Grand Canyon?

____

4. What do these rocks tell us?

____

____

Review

Directions: Skim the paragraph to answer this question.

1. What announcement is reported in the article?

____

Beginning Monday, drivers in northern Columbus may be facing more traffic jams. The Ohio Department of Transportation has announced that State Route 315 will be closed for repairs between Interstates 270 and 670. The closing will be in effect for the next three weeks. For alternate routes, drivers can use State Route 23 or Interstate 71.

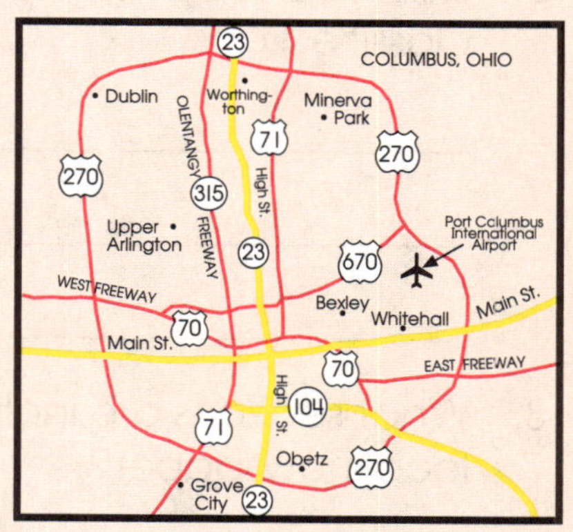

Directions: Skim the article to answer these questions.

1. What is the number of the highway that will be closed? __________

2. How long will the road closing be in effect? ____________________

Directions: Use the index to find the answers.

3. In which section of the paper would you find the announcement about the road closing?

____

4. On which page would you find tomorrow's forecast?

____

Business	8
Local News	5–7
Classified Ads	18–19
National News	1–4
Editorials	9
Sports	11–13
Entertainment	14–16
Weather	10

Directions: Read this classified ad. Then, answer the questions.

5. What facts are offered in the ad?

____

____

6. What opinion is offered in the ad?

____

____

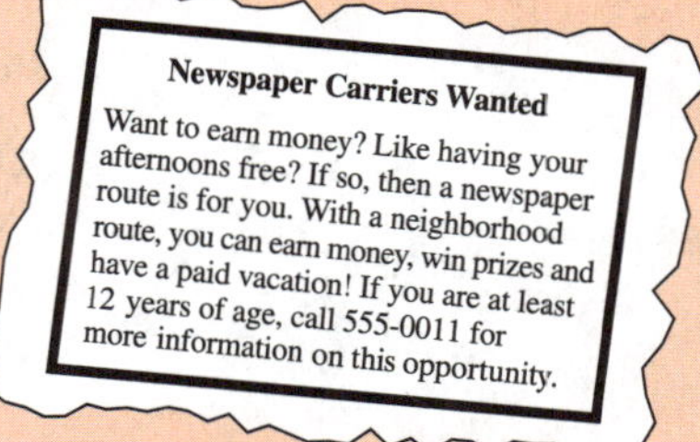

Newspaper Carriers Wanted

Want to earn money? Like having your afternoons free? If so, then a newspaper route is for you. With a neighborhood route, you can earn money, win prizes and have a paid vacation! If you are at least 12 years of age, call 555-0011 for more information on this opportunity.

Review

Directions: Write the answers.

1. What is the purpose of a classified ad?

2. Skim your local newspaper. List at least six categories of classified ads.

3. What sections are included in the index of your local newspaper?

4. What four pieces of information should a television program schedule contain?

5. What information is present on a medicine bottle?

6. Why is it important for medicine labels to include warnings?

Recognizing Details: The Coldest Continent

Directions: Read the information about Antarctica. Then, answer the questions.

Antarctica lies at the South Pole and is the coldest continent. It is without sunlight for months at a time. Even when the sun does shine, its angle is so slanted that the land receives little warmth. Temperatures often drop to 100 degrees below zero, and a fierce wind blows almost endlessly. Most of the land is covered by snow heaped thousands of feet deep. The snow is so heavy and tightly packed that it forms a great ice cap covering more than 95 percent of the continent.

Considering the conditions, it is no wonder there are no towns or cities in Antarctica. There is no permanent population at all, only small scientific research stations. Many teams of explorers and scientists have braved the freezing cold since Antarctica was sighted in 1820. Some have died in their effort, but a great deal of information has been learned about the continent.

From fossils, pieces of coal, and bone samples, we know that Antarctica was not always an ice-covered land. Scientists believe that 200 million years ago it was connected to southern Africa, South America, Australia, and India. Forests grew in warm swamps, and insects and reptiles thrived there. Today, there are animals that live in and around the waters that border the continent. In fact, the waters surrounding Antarctica contain more life than oceans in warmer areas of the world.

1. Where is Antarctica?

   ____

2. How much of the continent is covered by an ice cap?

   ____

3. When was Antarctica first sighted by explorers?

   ____

4. What clues indicate that Antarctica was not always an ice-covered land?

   ____

Reading Comprehension: The Arctic Circle

Directions: Read the article about the Arctic Circle. Then, answer the questions.

On the other side of the globe from Antarctica, at the northernmost part of Earth, is another icy land. This is the Arctic Circle. It includes the North Pole itself and the northern fringes of three continents—Europe, Asia, and North America, including the state of Alaska—as well as Greenland and other islands.

The seasons are opposite at the two ends of Earth. When it is summer in Antarctica, it is winter in the Arctic Circle. In both places, there are very long periods of sunlight in summer and very long nights in the winter. On the poles themselves, there are six full months of sunlight and six full months of darkness each year.

Compared to Antarctica, the summers are surprisingly mild in some areas of the Arctic Circle. Much of the snow cover may melt, and temperatures often reach 50 degrees in July. Antarctica is covered by water—frozen water, of course—so nothing can grow there. Plant growth is limited in the polar regions not only by the cold, but also by wind, lack of water, and the long winter darkness.

In the far north, willow trees grow but only become a few inches high! The annual rings, the circles within the trunk of a tree that show its age and how fast it grows, are so narrow that you need a microscope to see them.

A permanently frozen layer of soil, called **permafrost**, keeps roots from growing deep enough into the ground to anchor a plant. Even if a plant could survive the cold temperatures, it could not grow roots deep enough or strong enough to allow the plant to get very big.

1. What three continents have land included in the Arctic Circle?

   ____

   ____

   ____

2. Is the Arctic Circle generally warmer or colder than Antarctica?

   ____

3. What is **permafrost**? ______________________________

   ____

Main Idea: The Polar Trail

Directions: Read the information about explorers to Antarctica.

A recorded sighting of Antarctica, the last continent to be discovered, was not made until the early 19th century. Since then, many brave explorers and adventurers have sailed south to conquer the icy land. Their achievements once gained as much world attention as those of the first astronauts.

Long before the continent was first spotted, the ancient Greeks suspected there was a continent at the bottom of Earth. Over the centuries, legends of the undiscovered land spread. Some of the world's greatest seamen tried to find it, including Captain James Cook in 1772.

Cook was the first to sail all the way to the solid field of ice that surrounds Antarctica every winter. In fact, he sailed all the way around the continent but never saw it. Cook went farther south than anyone had ever gone. His record lasted 50 years.

Forty years after Cook, a new kind of seamen sailed the icy waters. They were hunters of seals and whales. Sailing through unknown waters in search of seals and whales, these men became explorers as well as hunters. The first person known to sight Antarctica was an American hunter, 21-year-old Nathaniel Brown Palmer in 1820.

Directions: Draw a ✓ in the box for the correct answer.

1. The main idea is:
   - ❑ Antarctica was not sighted until the early nineteenth century.
   - ❑ Many brave explorers and adventurers have sailed south to conquer the icy land.
2. The first person to sail to the ice field that surrounds Antarctica was:
   - ❑ Nathaniel Brown Palmer
   - ❑ Captain James Cook
   - ❑ Neal Armstrong
3. The first person known to sight Antarctica was:
   - ❑ an unknown ancient Greek
   - ❑ Captain James Cook
   - ❑ Nathaniel Brown Palmer
4. His profession was:
   - ❑ hunter
   - ❑ ship captain
   - ❑ explorer

Recognizing Details: The Frozen Continent

Directions: Read the information about explorers. Then, answer the questions.

By the mid-1800s, most of the seals of Antarctica had been killed. The seal hunters no longer sailed the icy waters. The next group of explorers who took an interest in Antarctica were scientists. Of these, the man who took the most daring chances and made the most amazing discoveries was British Captain James Clark Ross.

Ross first made a name for himself sailing to the north. In 1831, he discovered the North Magnetic Pole—one of two places on Earth toward which a compass needle points. In 1840, Ross set out to find the South Magnetic Pole. He made many marvelous discoveries, including the Ross Sea, a great open sea beyond the ice packs that stopped other explorers, and the Ross Ice Shelf, a great floating sheet of ice bigger than all of France!

The next man to make his mark exploring Antarctica was British explorer Robert Falcon Scott. Scott set out in 1902 to find the South Pole. He and his team suffered greatly, but they were able to make it a third of the way to the pole. Back in England, Scott was a great hero. In 1910, he again attempted to become the first man to reach the South Pole. But this time he had competition: an explorer from Norway, Roald Amundsen, was also leading a team to the South Pole.

It was a brutal race. Both teams faced many hardships, but they pressed on. Finally, on December 14, 1911, Amundsen became the first man to reach the South Pole. Scott arrived on January 17, 1912. He was bitterly disappointed at not being first. The trip back was even more horrible. None of the five men in the Scott expedition survived.

1. After the seal hunters, who were the next group of explorers interested in Antarctica?

   ____

2. What great discovery did James Ross make before ever sailing to Antarctica?

   ____

3. What were two other great discoveries made by James Ross?

   _______________ _______________

4. Who was the first person to reach the South Pole?

   ____

Reading Skills: Research

To learn more about the explorers to Antarctica, reference sources like encyclopedias, CD-ROMs, the Internet, and history books are excellent sources for finding more information.

Directions: Use reference sources to learn more about Captain James Cook and Captain James Clark Ross. Write an informational paragraph about each man.

1. Captain James Cook

____

____

____

____

____

2. Captain James Clark Ross

____

____

____

____

____

3. What dangers did both these men and their teams face in their attempts to reach the South Pole?

____

____

____

____

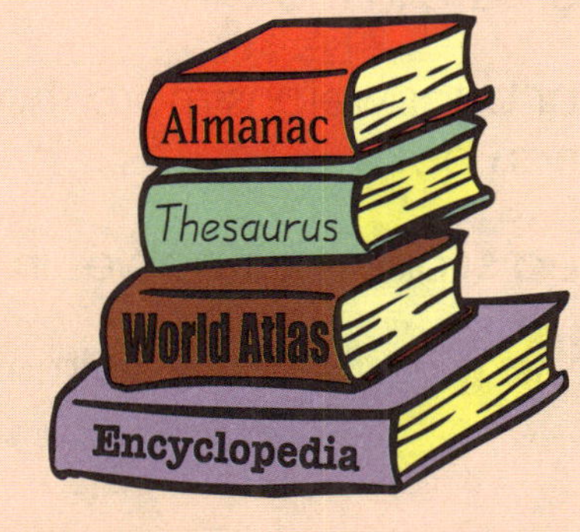

Reading Comprehension: Polar Bears

Directions: Read the information about polar bears. Then, answer the questions by circling **Yes** or **No**.

Some animals are able to survive the cold weather and difficult conditions of the snow and ice fields in the Arctic polar regions. One of the best known is the polar bear.

Polar bears live on the land and the sea. They may drift hundreds of miles from land on huge sheets of floating ice. They use their great paws to paddle the ice along. Polar bears are excellent swimmers, too. They can cross great distances of open water. While in the water, they feed mostly on fish and seals.

On land, these huge animals, which measure 10 feet long and weigh about 1,000 pounds, can run 25 miles an hour. Surprisingly, polar bears live as plant-eaters rather than hunters while on land. Unlike many kinds of bears, polar bears do not hibernate. They are active the whole year.

Baby polar bears are born during the winter. At birth, they are pink and almost hairless. These helpless cubs weigh only two pounds—less than one-third the size of most human infants. The mother bears raise their young in dens dug in snowbanks. By the time they are 10 weeks old, polar bear cubs are about the size of puppies and have enough white fur to protect them in the open air. The mothers give their cubs swimming, hunting, and fishing lessons. By the time autumn comes, the cubs are left to survive on their own.

1. Polar bears can live on the land and the sea. Yes No
2. Polar bears are excellent swimmers. Yes No
3. Polar bears hibernate in the winter. Yes No
4. A newborn polar bear weighs more than a newborn human baby. Yes No
5. Mother polar bears raise their babies in caves. Yes No
6. Father polar bears give the cubs swimming lessons. Yes No

Context Clues: Seals

Directions: Read the information about seals. Use context clues to determine the meaning of the bold words. Check the correct answers.

Seals are **aquatic** mammals that also live on land at times. Some seals stay in the sea for weeks or months at a time, even sleeping in the water. When seals go on land, they usually choose **secluded** spots to avoid people and other animals.

The 31 different kinds of seals belong to a group of animals often called pinnipeds meaning *fin-footed*. Their fins, or flippers, make them very good swimmers and divers. Their nostrils close tightly when they dive. They have been known to stay **submerged** for as long as a half-hour at a time!

Seals are warm-blooded animals that can adjust to various temperatures. They live in both **temperate** and cold climates. Besides their fur to keep them warm, seals have a thick layer of fat called blubber to protect them against the cold. It is harder for seals to cool themselves in hot weather than to warm themselves in cold weather. They can sometimes become so overheated that they die.

1. Based on other words in the sentence, what is the correct definition of **aquatic**?
   - ❑ living on the land
   - ❑ living on or in the sea
   - ❑ living in large groups
2. Based on other words in the sentence, what is the correct definition of **secluded**?
   - ❑ rocky
   - ❑ private or hidden
   - ❑ near other animals
3. Based on other words in the sentence, what is the correct definition of **submerged**?
   - ❑ under the water
   - ❑ on top of the water
   - ❑ in groups
4. Based on other words in the sentence, what is the correct definition of **temperate**?
   - ❑ rainy
   - ❑ measured on a thermometer
   - ❑ warm

Reading Comprehension: Walruses

Directions: Read the information about walruses. Then, answer the questions.

A walrus is actually a type of seal that lives only in the Arctic Circle. It has two huge upper teeth, or tusks, which it uses to pull itself out of the water or to move over the rocks on land. It also uses its tusks to dig clams, one of its favorite foods, from the bottom of the sea. On an adult male walrus, the tusks may be three and a half feet long!

A walrus has an unusual face. Besides its long tusks, it has a big, bushy mustache made up of hundreds of movable, stiff bristles. These bristles also help the walrus push food into its mouth. Except for small wrinkles in the skin, a walrus has no outer ears.

Like a seal, the walrus uses its flippers to help it swim. Its front flippers serve as paddles, and while swimming, it swings the back of its huge body from side to side. A walrus looks awkward using its flippers to walk on land, but don't be fooled! A walrus can run as fast as a man.

Baby walruses are born in the early spring. They stay with their mothers until they are two years old. There is a good reason for this—they must grow little tusks, at least three or four inches long, before they can catch their own food from the bottom of the sea. Until then, they must stay close to their mothers to eat. A young walrus that is tired from swimming will climb onto its mother's back for a ride, holding onto her with its front flippers.

1. The walrus is a type of seal found only

   ______________________________.

2. List two ways the walrus uses its tusks.

   ______________ ______________

3. A walrus cannot move quickly on land. Yes No

4. A walrus has a large, bushy mustache. Yes No

5. A baby walrus stays very close to its mother until it is two years old. Yes No

Main Idea: Penguins

Directions: Read the information about penguins.

People are amused by the funny, duck-like waddle of penguins and by their appearance because they seem to be wearing little tuxedos. Penguins are among the best-liked animals on Earth, but are also a most misunderstood animal. People may have more wrong ideas about penguins than any other animal.

For example, many people are surprised to learn that penguins are really birds, not mammals. Penguins do not fly, but they do have feathers, and only birds have feathers. Also, like other birds, penguins build nests and their young hatch from eggs. Because of their unusual looks, though, you would never confuse them with any other bird!

Penguins are also thought of as symbols of the polar regions, but penguins do not live north of the equator, so you would not find a penguin on the North Pole. Penguins don't live at the South Pole, either. Only two of the 17 **species** of penguins spend all of their lives on the frozen continent of Antarctica. You would be just as likely to see a penguin living on an island in a warm climate as in a cold area.

Directions: Draw a ✓ in the box for the correct answer.

1. The main idea is:
   - ❑ Penguins are among the best-liked animals on Earth.
   - ❑ The penguin is a much misunderstood animal.
2. Penguins live
   - ❑ only at the North Pole.
   - ❑ only at the South Pole.
   - ❑ only south of the equator.
3. Based on the other words in the sentence, what is the correct definition of the word **species**?
   - ❑ number
   - ❑ bird
   - ❑ a distinct kind

Review

Directions: Write a three-sentence summary for each of these selections. Refer to the reading selections for review if necessary.

1. "The Polar Trail"

____

____

____

2. "Polar Bears"

____

____

____

3. "Walruses"

____

____

____

Directions: Write the main idea of these selections. Refer to the reading selections for review if necessary.

4. "The Frozen Continent"

____

____

____

____

5. "Seals"

____

____

____

____

Review

Directions: Write your answers on the lines.

1. Which contains the South Pole—the Arctic or Antarctica?

2. Would you like to live in either the Arctic or Antarctica? Why or why not?

3. What adaptations would people who live (even for a short time) in these areas have to make?

4. What characteristics are common to animals who live in the polar regions?

5. Name two animals that live in the polar regions.

6. Write three facts you learned about one of the animals that live in the polar regions.

7. On each of the poles, there are six months of sunlight and six months of darkness each year. How do you think this would this affect you?

Reading Comprehension: The Desert

Directions: Read the information about the desert. Then, answer the questions by circling **Yes** or **No**.

Deserts are found where there is little rainfall or where the rainfall for a whole year falls in only a few weeks' time. Ten inches of rain may be enough for many plants to survive if the rain is spread throughout the year. If the 10 inches of rain falls during one or two months and the rest of the year is dry, those plants may not be able to survive and a desert may form.

When people think of deserts, they may think of long stretches of sand. Sand begins as tiny pieces of rock that get smaller and smaller as wind and weather wear them down. Sand dunes, or hills of drifting sand, are formed as winds move the sand across the desert. Grain by grain, the dunes grow over the years, always shifting with the winds and changing shape. Most dunes are only a few feet tall, but they can grow to be several hundred feet high.

There is, however, much more to a desert than sand. In the deserts of the southwestern United States, cliffs and canyons were formed from thick mud that once lay beneath a sea more than a hundred million years ago. Over the centuries, the water drained away. Wind, sand, rain, heat, and cold all wore away at the remaining rocks. The faces of the desert mountains are always changing—very, very slowly—as these forces of nature continue to work on the rock.

1. Deserts are found where there is little rainfall or where the rainfall for a whole year falls in only a few weeks. Yes No
2. Sand begins as tiny pieces of rock that get smaller and smaller as wind and weather wear them down. Yes No
3. Sand dunes were formed from thick mud that once lay beneath a sea more than a hundred million years ago. Yes No
4. The faces of the desert mountains can never change. Yes No

Reading Comprehension: Desert Weather

Directions: Read the information about desert weather. Then, answer the questions.

One definition of a desert is an area that has, on average, less than 10 inches of rain a year. Many deserts have far less than that. Death Valley in California and Nevada, for example, averages fewer than two inches of rain each year. The driest of all deserts is the Atacama Desert in Chile, where no rain has been known to fall in 400 years!

Some deserts have a regular rainy season each year, but usually desert rainfall is totally unpredictable. An area may have no rainfall for many years. Sometimes a passing cloud may look like it will send relief to the waiting land, but only a **ghost rain** falls. This means that the hot, dry air dries up the raindrops long before they ever reach the ground.

The temperature in the desert varies greatly. The daytime temperatures in the desert frequently top 120 degrees. In Death Valley, temperatures have been known to reach 190 degrees! In most parts of the world, moisture in the air works like a blanket to hold the heat of the day close to Earth at night. But, because it has so little moisture, the desert has no such blanket. As a result, nighttime temperatures are very chilly. Temperatures have been known to drop 50 or even 100 degrees at night in the desert.

1. On the average, how much rainfall is there in a year in a desert?

____

2. Where is the driest desert in the world?

____

3. What is a **ghost rain**?

____

4. In other parts of the world, what works as a blanket to hold the heat of the day close to Earth at night?

____

Review

Directions: Write a three-sentence summary of these selections which includes the main idea.

1. "The Desert"

____

____

____

____

2. "Desert Weather"

____

____

____

____

Directions: Define these words. Then, use them in sentences of your own.

3. dunes ____

____

4. canyon ____

____

5. average ____

____

6. unpredictable ____

____

Context Clues: Desert Plants

Directions: Read the information about desert plants. Use context clues to determine the meaning of the bold words. Check the correct answers.

Desert plants have special features, or adaptations, that allow them to **survive** the harsh conditions of the desert. A cactus stores water in its tissues when it rains. It then uses this supply of water during the long dry season. The tiny needles on some kinds of **cacti** may number in the tens of thousands. These sharp thorns protect the cactus. They also form tiny shadows in the sunlight that help keep the plant from getting too hot.

Other plants are able to live by dropping their leaves. This cuts down on the **evaporation** of their water supply in the hot sun. Still other plants survive as seeds, protected from the sun and heat by tough seed coats. When it rains, the seeds **sprout** quickly, bloom, and produce more seeds that can **withstand** long dry spells.

Some plants spread their roots close to Earth's surface to quickly gather water when it does rain. Other plants, such as the mesquite, have roots that grow 50 or 60 feet below the ground to reach underground water supplies.

1. Based on the other words in the sentence, what is the correct definition of **survive**?
   - ❑ continue to live
   - ❑ bloom in the desert
   - ❑ flower
2. Based on the other words in the sentence, what is the correct definition of **evaporation**?
   - ❑ water loss from heat
   - ❑ much-needed rainfall
   - ❑ boiling
3. Based on the other words in the sentence, what is the correct definition of **withstand**?
   - ❑ put up with
   - ❑ stand with another
   - ❑ take from
4. Based on the other words in the sentence, what is the correct definition of **cacti**?
   - ❑ a type of sand dune
   - ❑ more than one cactus
   - ❑ a caravan of camels
5. Based on the other words in the sentence, what is the correct definition of **sprout**?
   - ❑ a type of bean that grows only in the desert
   - ❑ begin to grow
   - ❑ a small flower

Recognizing Details: The Cactus Family

Directions: Read the information about cacti. Pay close attention to details. Answer the questions.

Although cacti are the best-known desert plants, they don't live only in hot, dry places. While cacti are most likely to be found in the desert areas of Mexico and the southwestern United States, they can by seen as far north as Nova Scotia, Canada. Certain types of cactus can live even in the snow!

Desert cactus are particularly good at surviving very long dry spells. Most cacti have a very long root system so they can absorb as much water as possible. Every available drop of water is taken into the cactus and held in its fleshy stem. A cactus stem can hold enough water to last for two years or longer.

A cactus may be best known for its spines. Although a few kinds of cacti don't have spines, the stems of most types are covered with these sharp needles. The spines have many uses for a cactus. They keep animals from eating the cactus. They collect raindrops and dew. The spines also help keep the plant cool by forming shadows in the sun and by trapping a layer of air close to the plant. They break up the desert winds that dry out the cactus.

Cacti come in all sizes and shapes. The biggest type in North America is the saguaro. It can weigh 12,000 to 14,000 pounds and grow to be 50 feet tall. A saguaro can last several years without water, but it will grow only after summer rains. In May and June, white blossoms appear. Many kinds of birds nest in these enormous cacti: white-winged doves, woodpeckers, small owls, thrashers, and wrens all build nests in the saguaro.

1. Where are you most likely to find a cactus growing?

   ____

2. How long can most cacti survive without water?

   ____

3. What are two ways the spines help a cactus?

   ____

   ____

4. What animals live in a saguaro cactus?

   ____

Review

Directions: Write a three-sentence summary of these selections. Refer to the reading selections for review if necessary.

1. "Desert Plants"

2. "The Cactus Family"

Directions: Describe the adaptations these plants have made to survive in the desert.

3. cacti
4. mesquite
5. saguaro cactus

Directions: Answer these questions.

6. What is the purpose of cactus spines?
7. Why does the mesquite have long roots?

Directions: Define these words. Then, use them in sentences of your own.

8. evaporation
9. spine

Reading Comprehension: Lizards

Directions: Read the information about lizards. Then, answer the questions.

Lizards are reptiles, related to snakes, turtles, alligators, and crocodiles. Like other reptiles, lizards are cold-blooded. This means their body temperature changes with that of their surroundings. However, by changing their behavior throughout the day, they can keep their temperature fairly constant.

Lizards are among the many animals that live in deserts. They usually come out of their burrows early in the morning. Most lizards lie in the sun to get warm before starting their daily activities. In mid-morning, they hunt for food. If it becomes too hot, lizards can raise their tails and bodies off the ground to help cool off. At mid-day, they return to their burrows or crawl under rocks for several hours. Late in the day, they again lie in the sun to absorb heat before the chilly desert night falls.

Like all animals, lizards have ways of protecting themselves. Some types of lizards have developed a most unusual defense. If a hawk or other animal grabs one of these lizards by its tail, the tail will break off. The tail will continue to wiggle around to distract the attacker while the lizard runs away. A month or two later, the lizard grows a new tail.

There are about 3,000 kinds of lizards, and all of them can bite, but only two types of lizards are poisonous: the Gila monster of the southwestern United States and the Mexican bearded lizard. Both are short-legged, thick-bodied reptiles with fat tails. These lizards do not attack people and will not bite them unless they are attacked.

1. What can a lizard do if it becomes too hot?

   ____

   ____

2. What is an unusual defense some lizards have developed to protect themselves?

   ____

3. What two types of lizards are poisonous?

   ____

   ____

Main Idea: People in the Desert

Directions: Read the information about people in the desert. Then, answer the questions.

Long before Europeans came to live in America, Native Americans had discovered ways of living in the desert. Some of these Native Americans were hunters or belonged to wandering tribes that stayed in the desert for only short periods of time. Others learned to farm and live in villages. They made their houses of trees, clay, and brush.

The desert met all of their needs for life: food, water, skins for clothing, materials for tools, weapons, and shelter. For meat, the desert offered deer, birds, and rabbits for hunting. When these animals were hard to find, the Native Americans would eat mice and lizards. Many desert plants, such as the prickly pear and mesquite, provided moisture, fruit, and seeds that could be eaten.

The first Europeans in the American deserts were searching for furs and metals, like silver and gold. They explored, but did not settle in the desert. The early pioneers were usually unsuccessful at living in the desert. They found the great heat and long dry periods too difficult. When they moved away, they left behind empty mining camps, houses, and sheds that slowly fell apart in the sun and wind.

1. What is the main idea of this selection?
   - ❑ Before Europeans came to live in America, Native Americans had discovered ways of successfully living in the desert.
   - ❑ Some Native Americans were hunters or belonged to wandering tribes who stayed in the desert for only short periods of time.

2. Who were the first people to live in the deserts of North America?

   ____

3. What kinds of food did the Native Americans find in the desert?

   ____

4. What were the first Europeans who came to the desert looking for?

   ____

Main Idea: Camels

Directions: Read the information about camels. Then, answer the questions.

Camels are well suited to desert life. They can cope with infrequent supplies of food and water, blazing heat during the day, low temperatures at night, and sand blown by high winds.

There are two kinds of camels: the two-humped bactrian and the one-humped dromedary. The dromedary is the larger of the two. It has coarse fur on its back that helps protect it from the sun's rays. The hair on its stomach and legs is short to prevent overheating. When camels **molt** in the spring, their wool can be collected in tufts from the bushes and ground.

The legs of the dromedary are much longer than those of the bactrian. Animals that live in very hot countries tend to have longer legs. This gives them a larger area of body surface from which heat can escape. Bactrian camels live in the deserts of central Asia where winters are bitterly cold, so they are not as tall as dromedaries.

Both kinds of camels have pads on their feet that keep them from sinking into the sand as they walk. A camel's long neck allows it to reach the ground to drink water and eat grass without having to bend its legs. It also can reach up to eat leaves from trees.

Camels do not store water in their humps as many people believe. The hump is for fat storage. When there is plenty of food, the camel's hump swells and feels firm. During the dry season when there is little food, the fat is used up and the hump shrinks and becomes soft.

1. What is the main idea of this selection?
   - ❑ Camels are well suited to desert life.
   - ❑ There are two kinds of camels.
2. Based on the other words in the sentence, what is the correct definition of **molt**?
   - ❑ turns into a butterfly
   - ❑ sheds its hair
   - ❑ becomes overheated
3. What are the two kinds of camels?

   ____

4. Why don't camels sink into the sand when they walk?

   ____

Review

Directions: Write your answers in complete sentences.

1. Describe how the cold-blooded lizard regulates its body temperature.

2. What is the main idea of the selection "Lizards"?

3. Describe how Native Americans adapted to life in the desert.

4. Why do you think early pioneers were unsuccessful at desert living?

5. Describe the adaptations of camels for successful desert habitation.

Review

Directions: Define each of these words. Use them in sentences of your own.

1. desert ______________________________

____

2. dune ______________________________

____

3. cactus ______________________________

____

4. evaporation ______________________________

____

5. withstand ______________________________

____

6. sprout ______________________________

____

7. survive ______________________________

____

8. saguaro ______________________________

____

9. mesquite ______________________________

____

10. dromedary ______________________________

____

Paraphrasing

To **paraphrase** means *to reword a passage so it is in your own words rather than the words of the author.*

Example:

Original: The cat and dog regularly raced to greet their owners at the front door.

Paraphrased: Upon returning home, the owners always found their dog and cat waiting anxiously by the front door.

Directions: Paraphrase these paragraphs.

1. "The Desert": paragraph 1

____

____

____

____

2. "Desert Weather": paragraph 3

____

____

____

____

3. "The Cactus Family": paragraph 3

____

____

____

____

Reading Comprehension: Desert Lakes

Directions: Read the information about lakes in the desert. Then, answer the questions.

A few deserts have small permanent lakes. While they may be a welcome sight in the desert, the water in them is not fit for drinking. They are salt lakes. Rain from nearby higher land keeps these lakes supplied with water, but the lakes are blocked in with nowhere to drain. Over the years, mineral salts collect in the water and build up to a high level, making the water undrinkable.

Most desert lakes are only temporary. Occasional rains may fill them to depths of several feet, but in a matter of weeks or months, all the water has been dried up by the heat and sun. The dried lake beds that remain are called **playas**. Some playas are simply areas of sun-baked mud; others are covered with a sparkling layer of salt.

Perhaps the most unusual desert lake is in central Australia. It is called Lake Eyre. It is a huge lake—nearly 3,600 square miles in area—but it is almost totally dry most of the time. Since it was discovered in 1840, it has been filled only two times. Both times, the lake completely dried up again within a few years.

1. Why is the water in a desert lake not fit for drinking?

 ____

2. Why are the lakes in the desert salt lakes?

 ____

3. Why are most desert lakes only temporary?

 ____

4. What is a **playa**? ______________________________

5. What is the name of the unusual desert lake in central Australia?

 ____

Review

Directions: Write your answers in complete sentences.

1. What is a desert?

____

____

2. Name a desert in the United States and tell where it is.

____

____

3. What special characteristics must an animal have to survive in the desert?

____

____

____

4. What special characteristics must a plant have to survive in the desert?

____

____

____

5. Would you like to visit the desert? Why or why not?

____

____

____

____

____

Reading Comprehension: Railroads

Directions: Read the information about railroads. Then, answer the questions.

As early as the 1550s, a rough form of railroad was already being used in parts of Europe. Miners in England and other areas of western Europe used horse- or mule-drawn wagons on wooden tracks to pull loads out of mines. With these tracks, the horses could pull twice as much weight as they could without them. No one could have known then that one day this simple idea would change the world.

There were many developments along the way that helped make railroads a practical and valuable form of transportation. Two of the most important were the iron track and the "flanged" wheel, which has a rim around it to hold it onto the track. The most important invention was the steam engine by James Watt in 1765.

The first railroads in the United States were built during the late 1820s and caused a lot of excitement. They were faster than other forms of travel, and they could provide service year-round, unlike boats and stagecoaches. Trains were soon the main means of travel in the U.S.

Railroads played a major part in the Industrial Revolution—the years of change when machines were first used to do work that had been done by hand for many centuries. Trains provided cheaper rates and quicker service for transporting goods. Because manufacturers could ship their goods over long distances, they could sell their products all over the nation instead of only in the surrounding cities and towns. This meant greater profits for the companies. Trains also brought people into the cities to work in factories.

1. What was the source of power for the earliest railroads?

____

2. What were three important developments that made railroads a practical means of transportation?

____

____

____

3. What is meant by the Industrial Revolution? ____________________

____

Main Idea: Locomotives

Directions: Read the information about locomotives. Then, answer the questions.

In the 1800s, the steam locomotive was considered by many to be a symbol of the new Industrial Age. It was, indeed, one of the most important inventions of the time. Over the years, there have been many changes to the locomotive. One of the most important has been its source of power. During its history, the locomotive has gone from steam to electric to diesel power.

The first railroads used horses or mules for power, but the development of the steam locomotive made railroads a practical means of transportation. The first steam locomotive was built in 1804 in Great Britain by Richard Trevithick. It could haul 50,000 pounds, but it was not very successful because it was so heavy it caused the tracks to fall apart. However, it encouraged other engineers to try to build steam locomotives. Two of the most important men to accept the challenge were George Stephenson and his son, Robert. Robert once won a contest to build the best locomotive. *The Rocket*, as he called it, had a top speed of 29 miles per hour.

In America, developments in steam engines were close behind those of the British. In 1830, Peter Cooper's tiny locomotive, called *Tom Thumb*, lost a famous race against a horse-drawn coach. In spite of the loss, it still convinced railroad officials that steam power was more practical than horsepower.

Just before the turn of the century, the electric locomotive was widely used. At its peak in the 1940s, U.S. railroads had 2,400 miles of electric routes.

The diesel locomotive was invented in the 1890s by Rudolf Diesel, a German engineer. The power of this locomotive was supplied by a diesel fuel engine. The diesel locomotive is still used today. It costs about twice as much as a steam locomotive to build, but it is much cheaper to operate.

1. What is the main idea of this selection?
   - ❑ The steam locomotive was considered a symbol of the Industrial Age.
   - ❑ Over the years, there have been many changes to the locomotive.

2. Who built the first steam locomotive in 1804?

   ____

3. How fast could *The Rocket* travel?

   ____

Review

Directions: Define these words as used in the selections "Railroads" and "Locomotives."

1. flanged wheel ______________________________

____

2. transportation ______________________________

____

3. profit ______________________________

____

4. locomotive ______________________________

____

5. diesel ______________________________

____

6. engineer ______________________________

____

Directions: Write your answer in a complete sentence.

7. The world is going through another "revolution" in industry today. What new technology is leading this change and how might it affect workers in the future?

____

____

____

Reading Comprehension: Railroad Pioneer

Directions: Read the information about railroad pioneers. Then, answer the questions by circling **Yes** or **No**.

George Stephenson was born in Wylam, England, in 1781. His family was extremely poor. When he was young, he didn't go to school but worked in the coal mines. In his spare time, he taught himself to read and write. After a series of explosions in the coal pits, Stephenson built a miner's safety lamp. This helped bring him to the attention of the owners of the coal mines. They put him in charge of all the machinery.

In 1812, Stephenson became an engine builder for the mines. The owners were interested in locomotives because the cost of horse feed was so high. They wanted Stephenson to build a locomotive to pull the coal cars from the mines. His first locomotive, *The Blucher,* was put on the rails in 1814.

Stephenson was a good engineer, and he was fortunate to work for a rich employer. Between 1814 and 1826, Stephenson was the only man in Great Britain building locomotives.

When the Stockholm and Darlington Railway, the first public railroad system, was planned, Stephenson was named company engineer. He convinced the owners to use steam power instead of horses. He built the first locomotive on the line. *The Locomotion,* as it was called, was the best locomotive that had been built anywhere in the world up to that time. Over the years, Stephenson was responsible for many other important developments in locomotive design, such as improved cast-iron rails and wheels, and the first steel springs strong enough to carry several tons.

Stephenson was convinced that the future of railroads lay in steam power. His great vision of what the railroad system could become was a driving force in the early years of its development.

1. George Stephenson was an excellent student in school. Yes No
2. Stephenson's first invention was a miner's safety lamp. Yes No
3. Between 1814 and 1826, Stephenson was one of many engineers building locomotives in Great Britain. Yes No
4. The Stockholm and Darlington Railway was the first public railroad system. Yes No
5. The first locomotive on the Stockholm and Darlington line was *The Locomotion,* built by Stephenson. Yes No

Tall Tales

A **tall tale** is a fictional story with exaggerated details and a "super" hero. The main character in a tall tale is much larger, stronger, smarter, or better than a real person. Tall tales may be unbelievable, but they are fun to hear.

Directions: Read the story about John Henry. Then, answer the questions.

A Steel-Driving Man

On the night John Henry was born, forked lightning split the air and the earth shook. He weighed 44 pounds at birth, and the first thing he did was reach for a hammer hanging on the wall. "He's going to be a steel-driving man," his father told his mother.

One night, John Henry dreamed he was working on a railroad. Every time his hammer hit a spike, the sky lit up with the sparks. "I dreamed that the railroad was going to be the end of me, and I'd die with a hammer in my hand," he said. When John Henry grew up he did work for the railroad. He was the fastest, most powerful steel-driving man in the world.

In about 1870, the steam drill was invented. One day the company at the far end of a tunnel tried it out. John Henry's company, working at the other end, continued to use men to do the drilling. There was much bragging from both companies as to which was faster. Finally, they decided to have a contest. John Henry was matched against the best man with a steam drill.

John Henry swung a 20-pound hammer in each hand. The sparks flew so fast and hot that they burned his face. At the end of the day, the judges said John Henry had beaten the steam drill by four feet!

That night, John Henry said, "I was a steel-driving man." Then, he laid down and closed his eyes forever.

1. How much was John Henry said to have weighed at birth?

   ____

2. Why did his father think he would be a steel-driving man?

   ____

3. What invention was John Henry in a contest against? __________

4. Who won the contest? ______________________________

5. What happened to John Henry after the contest? __________

Tall Tales

Directions: Write a tall tale about yourself. Be sure to make it a fantastic and incredible story!

Directions: Reread your tall tale. Does it make sense? Check and correct spelling and grammar mistakes. Does your story fit the category of a tall tale?

Context Clues: Passenger Cars

Directions: Read the information about passenger cars. Use context clues to determine the meaning of words in bold. Check the correct answers.

Early railroad passenger cars were little more than stagecoaches fitted with special wheels to help them stay on the tracks. They didn't hold many passengers, and because they were made out of wood, they were fire hazards. They also did not hold up very well if the train came off the track or had a **collision** with another train.

In the United States, it wasn't long before passenger cars were lengthened to hold more people. Late in the 1830s, Americans were riding in **elongated** cars with double seats on either side of a center aisle. By the early 1900s, most cars were made of metal instead of wood.

Sleeping and dining cars were introduced in the United States by the early 1860s. Over the next 25 years other improvements were made, including electric lighting, steam heat, and covered **vestibules** that allowed passengers to walk between cars. All of these **luxuries** helped make railroad travel much more comfortable.

1. Based on the other words in the sentence, what is the correct definition of **collision**?
   - ❑ crash
   - ❑ race
   - ❑ track
2. Based on the other words in the sentence, what is the correct definition of **elongated**?
   - ❑ wooden
   - ❑ new
   - ❑ lengthened
3. Based on the other words in the sentence, what is the correct definition of **vestibules**?
   - ❑ passageways
   - ❑ cars
   - ❑ depots
4. Based on the other words in the sentence, what is the correct definition of **luxuries**?
   - ❑ additions
   - ❑ things offering the greatest comfort
   - ❑ inventions

Reading Skills: Railroads

Directions: Read the information about railroads. Then, answer the questions.

When railroads became the major means of transportation, they replaced earlier forms of travel, like the stagecoach. Railroads remained the unchallenged leader for a hundred years. Beginning in the early 1900s, railroads faced **competition** from newer forms of transportation.

Today, millions of people have their own automobiles. Buses offer inexpensive travel between cities. Large trucks haul goods across the country. Airplanes provide quick transportation over long distances. The result has been a sharp drop in the use of trains.

Today, nearly all railroads face serious problems that threaten to drive them out of business. But railroads still provide low-cost, fuel-saving transportation that will remain important. One gallon of diesel fuel will haul about four times as much by railroad as by truck. In a time when the world is concerned about saving fuel, this is one area in which the railroads still have much to offer.

1. What is the main idea of this selection?
   - ❑ When railroads became the major means of transportation, they replaced earlier forms of travel.
   - ❑ Beginning in the early 1900s, railroads have faced competition from newer forms of transportation.
2. Based on the other words in the sentence, what is the correct definition of **competition**?
   - ❑ businesses trying to get the same customers
   - ❑ problems
   - ❑ support
3. What are four newer forms of transportation that have challenged railroads?

   ____

Review

Directions: Write your answers in complete sentences.

1. Today, we have machines which are capable of putting in railroad tracks. However, in the 1800s, all the work was done by hand. What dangers and difficulties might railroad workers have faced?

____

____

____

____

2. Why was the railroad a major contributor to the Industrial Revolution?

____

____

____

____

3. Compare traveling by train to traveling by one other form of transportation, past or present. Discuss the advantages and disadvantages of both.

____

____

____

____

Author's Purpose

Authors write to fulfill one of three purposes: to **inform**, to **entertain**, or to **persuade**.

Authors who write to inform are providing facts for the reader in an informational context.

Examples: Encyclopedia entries and newspaper articles

Authors who write to entertain are hoping to provide enjoyment for the reader.

Examples: Funny stories and comics

Authors who write to persuade are trying to convince the reader to believe as they believe.

Examples: Editorials and opinion essays

Directions: Read each paragraph. Write **inform**, **entertain**, or **persuade** on the line to show the author's purpose.

1. The whooping crane is a migratory bird. At one time, this endangered bird was almost extinct. These large white cranes are characterized by red faces and trumpeting calls. Through protection of both the birds and their habitats, the whooping crane is slowly increasing in number.

   ____

2. It is extremely important that all citizens place bird feeders in their yards and keep them full for the winter. Birds that spend the winter in this area are in danger of starving due to lack of food. It is every citizen's responsibility to ensure the survival of the birds.

   ____

3. Imagine being able to hibernate like a bear each winter! Wouldn't it be great to eat to your heart's content all fall? Then, sometime in late November, inform your teacher that you will not be attending school for the next few months because you'll be resting and living off your fat? Now, that would be the life!

   ____

Author's Purpose

Directions: Write a paragraph of your own for each purpose. The paragraph can be about any topic.

1. to inform

____

____

____

____

____

____

2. to persuade

____

____

____

____

____

____

3. to entertain

____

____

____

____

____

____

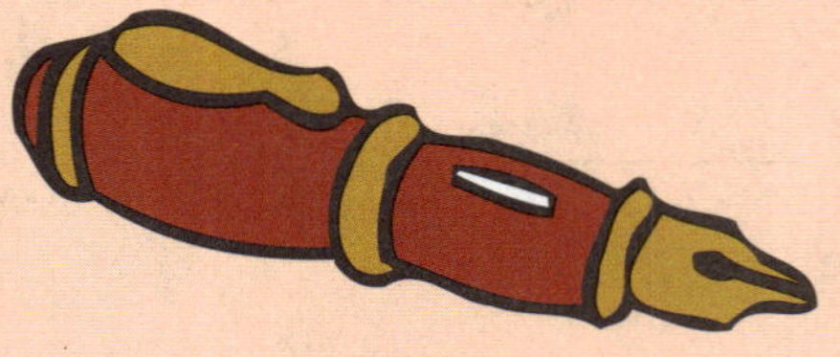

Reading a Recipe

Directions: Read the recipe. Then, answer the questions.

Graham Cracker Smoothies

Ingredients:

Graham crackers
For the icing:
2 T. peanut butter
2 T. butter
2 c. powdered sugar
milk

Break graham crackers in half. Mix peanut butter, butter, and powdered sugar with a spoon. Add enough milk to make creamy icing. Stir vigorously until no lumps remain. Spread on graham cracker half and top with another graham cracker half, sandwich style. Enjoy! The smoothie icing will keep in the refrigerator for two days.

1. What do these abbreviations stand for?

   T. ______________________________

   c. ______________________________

2. Number the steps in the correct order.

   ______ Spread icing on graham crackers.

   ______ Add milk and stir until creamy.

   ______ Break graham crackers in half.

   ______ Eat and enjoy.

   ______ Mix the peanut butter, butter, and powdered sugar together.

3. Why is it important to follow the correct sequence when cooking?

   ____

What's Your Opinion?

Most people have opinions about many topics. If you were asked how you felt about a certain sports team, an earlier bedtime, or a meal, you would give your opinion. Several times each day, people state an opinion about something and that opinion is unique to that individual. Although others may hold the same opinion, their reasons may be different.

When writing an opinion paragraph, begin by stating the topic and how you feel about it. In the next few sentences, support your opinion by giving reasons. Provide justification for why you believe as you do. Finally, complete the paragraph by restating your opinion in a conclusion sentence.

Example:

I believe that the minimum wage in the United States should be raised to $9.00 per hour. There are several reasons why I feel this way. Most importantly, at the current minimum wage, a worker would make under $15,000 per year working a 40-hour week. A person who is working full-time should be compensated at a wage which allows him or her to live comfortably. At the wage, of $9.00 per hour, a worker would make a little over $18,500 per year. For these reasons, I believe that raising the minimum wage to $9.00 per hour would be a benefit to workers everywhere.

Directions: Write an opinion essay for this topic.

A Minimum Grade of C for Sports Participation

Cumulative Review

Directions: Write the answers.

1. Give an example of a word with a prefix and define it.

   ____

2. Give an example of a word with a suffix and define it.

   ____

3. Define *simile* and give an example.

   ____

   ____

4. Define *metaphor* and give an example.

   ____

   ____

5. Define *idiom* and give an example.

   ____

   ____

   ____

Directions: Complete these analogies.

6. Car is to road as cup is to ____________________.
7. Rough is to smooth as above is to ____________________.
8. Handle is to teapot as frame is to ____________________.
9. Words are to book as flowers are to ____________________.

Cumulative Review

Directions: Write **F** if the sentence is a fact. Write **O** if it is an opinion.

1. ______ My dog is the most well-behaved on the block.
2. ______ Lake Erie is one of the Great Lakes.
3. ______ The Civil War began in 1861.
4. ______ Alaska has the most beautiful scenery.
5. ______ The Eiffel Tower is in Paris, France.
6. ______ The teacher grades unfairly.

Directions: Write your answers in complete sentences.

7. What is the purpose of skimming a selection?

____

____

8. What does the word *context* mean?

____

____

____

9. What are an author's three purposes when writing?

____

____

10. Write a set of directions for playing a sport or doing a hobby that you enjoy. Reread to be certain the directions make sense.

____

____

____

Personal Narratives

A **personal narrative** tells about a person's own experiences.

Directions: Read the example of a personal narrative. Write your answers in complete sentences.

My Worst Year

When I look back on that year, I can hardly believe that one person could have such terrible luck for a whole year. But then again, I should have realized that if things could begin to go wrong in January, it didn't bode well for the rest of the year.

It was the night of January 26. One of my best friends was celebrating her birthday at the local roller-skating rink, and I had been invited. The evening began well enough with pizza and laughs. I admit I have never been a cracker jack roller skater, but I could hold my own. After a few minutes of skating, I decided to exit the rink for a cold soda.

Unfortunately, I did not notice the trailing ribbons of carpet which wrapped around the wheel of my skate, yanking my left leg from under me. My leg was broken. It wasn't just broken in one place but in four places! At the hospital, the doctor set the bone and put a cast on my leg. Three months later, I felt like a new person.

Sadly, the happiness wasn't meant to last. Five short months after the final cast was removed, I fell and broke the same leg again. Not only did it rebreak but it broke in the same four places! We found out later that it hadn't healed correctly. Three months later, it was early December and the end of a year I did not wish to repeat.

1. List the sequence of events in this personal narrative.

____

____

____

____

2. From reading the personal narrative, what do you think were the author's feelings toward the events that occurred?

____

____

Personal Narratives

Directions: Using the personal narrative on the previous page as an example, write a narrative about an experience of your own. When you finish, remember to reread your narrative. Check for and correct spelling, grammar, and punctuation mistakes.

Complete the Story

Directions: Read the beginning of this story. Then, complete the story with your own ideas.

It was a beautiful summer day in June when my family and I set off on vacation. We were headed for Portsmouth, New Hampshire. There, we planned to go on a whale-watching ship and perhaps spy a humpback whale or two. However, there were many miles between our home and Portsmouth.

We camped at many lovely parks along the way to New Hampshire. We stayed in the Adirondack Mountains for a few days and then visited the White Mountains of Vermont before crossing into New Hampshire.

My family enjoys tent camping. My dad says you can't really get a taste of the great outdoors in a pop-up camper or RV. I love sitting by the fire at night, gazing at the stars, and listening to the animal noises.

The trip was going well, and everyone was enjoying our vacation. We made it to Portsmouth and were looking forward to the whale-watching adventure. We arrived at the dock a few minutes early. The ocean looked rough, but we had taken seasickness medication. We thought we were prepared for any kind of weather.

Glossary

Analogy: A way of comparing objects to show how they relate. Example: **Nose is to smell as tongue is to taste.**

Cause: An event or reason which has an effect on something else. Example: **The heavy rains produced flooding in Chicago.**

Classified Ad: An advertisement in a newspaper or magazine offering a product or service for sale or rent. Example: **For Sale. Used 26" 30-speed bike. $100. Call 555-5555.**

Classifying: Putting items into categories based on similar characteristics.

Context Clues: A way to figure out the meaning of a new word by relating it to the other words in the sentence.

Effect: An event that results from a cause. Example: **The flooding in Chicago was due to the heavy rains.**

Fact: Information that can be proved. Example: **Hawaii is a state**.

Homographs: Words that have the same spelling but different meanings and pronunciations. Example: **present** (a gift) and **present** (to introduce)

Homophones: Words that are pronounced the same but are spelled differently and have different meanings. Example: **forth** and **fourth**

Index: A listing in a book, magazine, or newspaper that tells where to find items or information.

Idiom: A phrase that says one thing but actually means something quite different. Example: **A horse of a different color** means something very strange or unusual.

Labels: Provide information about products.

Main Idea: The most important point in an article.

Metaphor: A direct comparison between two things. Example: **The sun is a yellow ball in the sky.**

Newspaper Index: A guide for where to find information in a newspaper.

Opinion: What someone thinks. It cannot be proved. Example: **Hawaii is the prettiest state.**

Paraphrase: To reword a passage so it is in your own words rather than the words of the author.

Glossary

Personal Narrative: Tells about a person's own experiences.

Prefix: A syllable at the beginning of a word that changes its meaning.

Root Word: A word that is the common stem that gives related words their basic meaning.

Schedule: A listing of events or programs by time, date, and place or channel.

Sequencing: To place events in order from beginning to end or first to last.

Simile: A comparison of two things that have something in common but are really very different. The words **like** and **as** are used in similes. Example: **The baby was as happy as a lark.**

Skimming: Reading quickly to get an overall idea of the content of an article or to find a particular fact.

Suffix: A syllable at the end of a word that changes its meaning.

Tall Tale: A fictional story with exaggerated details and a super hero.

Answer Key

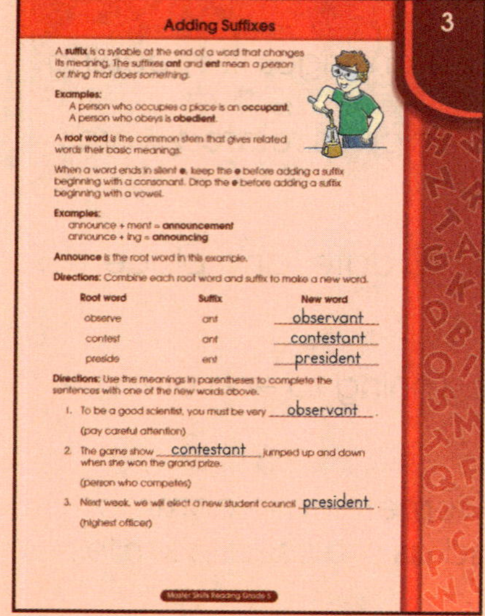

3

Adding Suffixes

A **suffix** is a syllable at the end of a word that changes its meaning. The suffixes **ant** and **ent** mean *a person or thing that does something.*

Examples:
A person who occupies a place is an **occupant**.
A person who obeys is **obedient**.

A **root word** is the common stem that gives related words their basic meanings.

When a word ends in silent **e**, keep the **e** before adding a suffix beginning with a consonant. Drop the **e** before adding a suffix beginning with a vowel.

Examples:
announce + ment = **announcement**
announce + ing = **announcing**

Announce is the root word in this example.

Directions: Combine each root word and suffix to make a new word.

Root word	Suffix	New word
observe	ant	observant
contest	ant	contestant
preside	ent	president

Directions: Use the meanings in parentheses to complete the sentences with one of the new words above.

1. To be a good scientist, you must be very observant.
(pay careful attention)
2. The game show contestant jumped up and down when she won the grand prize.
(person who competes)
3. Next week, we will elect a new student council president.
(highest officer)

Master Skills Reading Grade 5

3

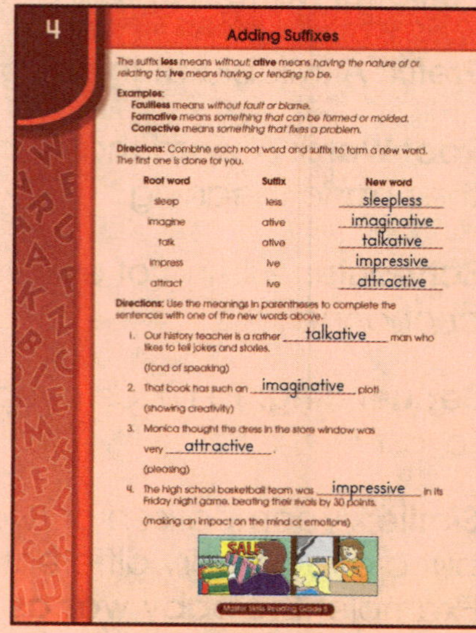

4

Adding Suffixes

The suffix **less** means *without*; **ative** means *having the nature of or relating to*; **ive** means *having or tending to be.*

Examples:
Faultless means *without fault or blame.*
Formative means *something that can be formed or molded.*
Corrective means *something that fixes a problem.*

Directions: Combine each root word and suffix to form a new word. The first one is done for you.

Root word	Suffix	New word
sleep	less	sleepless
imagine	ative	imaginative
talk	ative	talkative
impress	ive	impressive
attract	ive	attractive

Directions: Use the meanings in parentheses to complete the sentences with one of the new words above.

1. Our history teacher is a rather talkative man who likes to tell jokes and stories.
(fond of speaking)
2. That book has such an imaginative plot!
(showing creativity)
3. Monica thought the dress in the store window was very attractive.
(pleasing)
4. The high school basketball team was impressive in its Friday night game, beating their rivals by 30 points.
(making an impact on the mind or emotions)

Master Skills Reading Grade 5

4

5

Adding Prefixes

A **prefix** is a syllable at the beginning of a word that changes its meaning. The prefixes **il**, **im**, **in**, and **ir** all mean *not.*

Examples:
Illogical means *not logical or practical.*
Impossible means *not possible.*
Invisible means *not visible.*
Irrelevant means *not relevant or practical.*

Directions: Divide each word into its prefix and root word. The first one is done for you.

	Prefix	Root Word
illogical	il	logical
impatient	im	patient
immature	im	mature
incomplete	in	complete
insincere	in	sincere
irresponsible	ir	responsible
irregular	ir	regular

Directions: Use the meanings in parentheses to complete the sentences with one of the words above.

1. I had to turn in my assignment incomplete because I was sick last night.
(not finished)
2. Sue and Joel were irresponsible to leave their bikes out in the rain.
(not doing the right thing)
3. I sometimes get impatient waiting for my ride to school.
(restless)
4. The boys sounded insincere when they said they were sorry.
(not honest)
5. These towels didn't cost much because they are irregular.
(not straight or even)

Master Skills Reading Grade 5

5

6

Adding Prefixes

The prefix **pre** means *before*. The prefix **re** means *again.*

Examples:
Preview means *to see in advance.*
Redo means *to do again.*

PRE FIX

Directions: Write sentences using these words with prefixes.

1. prefix ______
2. redirect ______
3. regain ______
Answers will vary.
4. predetermine ______
5. reorganize ______
6. prepackage ______
7. redistribute ______

Master Skills Reading Grade 5

6

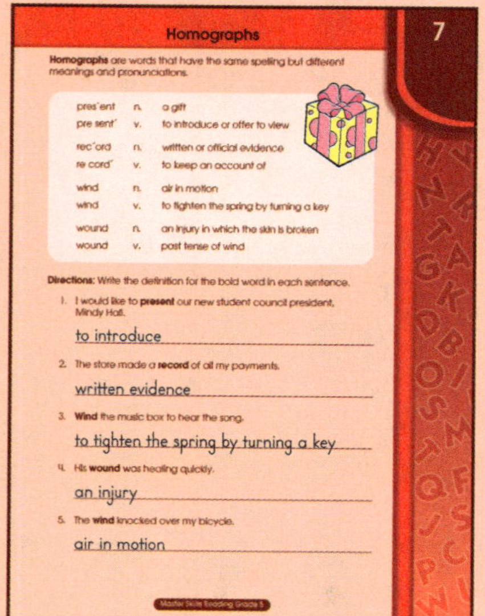

7

Homographs

Homographs are words that have the same spelling but different meanings and pronunciations.

pres´ ent	n.	a gift
pre sent´	v.	to introduce or offer to view
rec´ ord	n.	written or official evidence
re cord´	v.	to keep an account of
wind	n.	air in motion
wind	v.	to tighten the spring by turning a key
wound	n.	an injury in which the skin is broken
wound	v.	past tense of wind

Directions: Write the definition for the bold word in each sentence.

1. I would like to **present** our new student council president, Mindy Hall.
to introduce
2. The store made a **record** of all my payments.
written evidence
3. **Wind** the music box to hear the song.
to tighten the spring by turning a key
4. His **wound** was healing quickly.
an injury
5. The **wind** knocked over my bicycle.
air in motion

Master Skills Reading Grade 5

7

8

Homophones

Homophones are words that are pronounced the same but are spelled differently and have different meanings.

Example: to, two, too

to two too

Directions: Use these homophones in sentences of your own.

1. forth ______
2. fourth ______
3. they're ______
4. their ______ Answers will vary.
5. there ______
6. not ______
7. knot ______

Master Skills Reading Grade 5

8

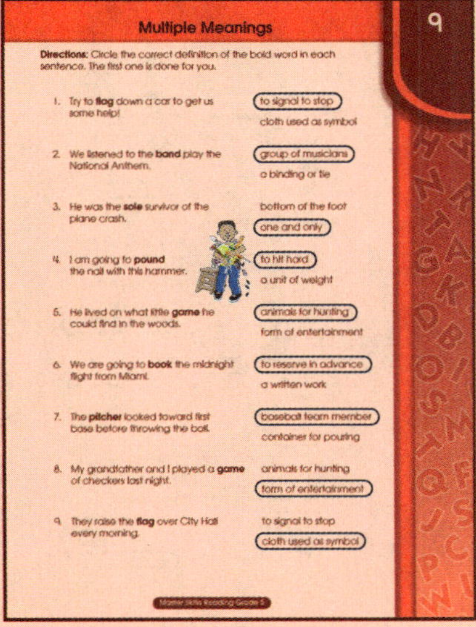

Multiple Meanings

Directions: Circle the correct definition of the bold word in each sentence. The first one is done for you.

1. Try to **flag** down a car to get us some help! — (to signal to stop) / cloth used as symbol
2. We listened to the **band** play the National Anthem. — (group of musicians) / a binding or tie
3. He was the **sole** survivor of the plane crash. — bottom of the foot / (one and only)
4. I am going to **pound** the nail with this hammer. — (to hit hard) / a unit of weight
5. He lived on what little **game** he could find in the woods. — (animals for hunting) / form of entertainment
6. We are going to **book** the midnight flight from Miami. — (to reserve in advance) / a written work
7. The **pitcher** looked toward first base before throwing the ball. — (baseball team member) / container for pouring
8. My grandfather and I played a **game** of checkers last night. — animals for hunting / (form of entertainment)
9. They raise the **flag** over City Hall every morning. — to signal to stop / (cloth used as symbol)

9

Similes

A **simile** is a comparison of two things that have something in common but are really very different. The words **like** and **as** are used in similes.

Examples:
The baby was as happy **as** a lark.
She is **like** a ray of sunshine to my tired eyes.

Directions: Choose a word from the box to complete each comparison. The first one is done for you.

tack grass fish mule ox monkey

1. as stubborn as a mule
2. as strong as an ox
3. swims like a fish
4. as sharp as a tack
5. climbs like a monkey
6. as green as grass

Directions: Use your own words to complete these similes.

7. ________ like a bird Answers will vary.
8. as hungry as a ________
9. as white as ________
10. as ________ as honey
11. ________ like a snake
12. as cold as ________

Directions: Use your own similes to complete these sentences.

13. Our new puppy sounded ________.
14. The clouds were ________.
15. The watermelon tasted ________.

10

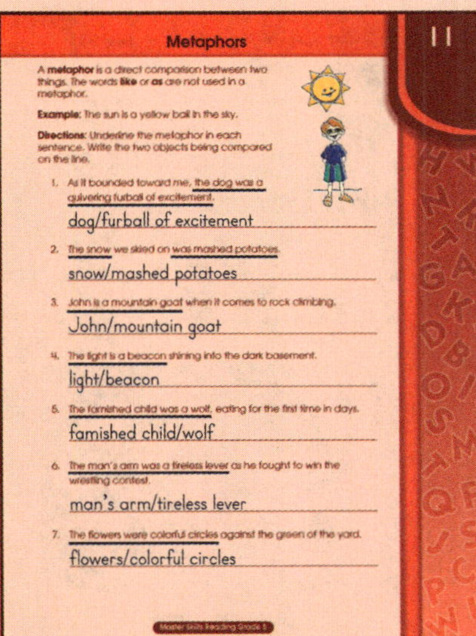

Metaphors

A **metaphor** is a direct comparison between two things. The words **like** or **as** are not used in a metaphor.

Example: The sun is a yellow ball in the sky.

Directions: Underline the metaphor in each sentence. Write the two objects being compared on the line.

1. As it bounded toward me, the dog was a quivering furball of excitement.
dog/furball of excitement
2. The snow we skied on was mashed potatoes.
snow/mashed potatoes
3. John is a mountain goat when it comes to rock climbing.
John/mountain goat
4. The light is a beacon shining into the dark basement.
light/beacon
5. The famished child was a wolf, eating for the first time in days.
famished child/wolf
6. The man's arm was a tireless lever as he fought to win the wrestling contest.
man's arm/tireless lever
7. The flowers were colorful circles against the green of the yard.
flowers/colorful circles

11

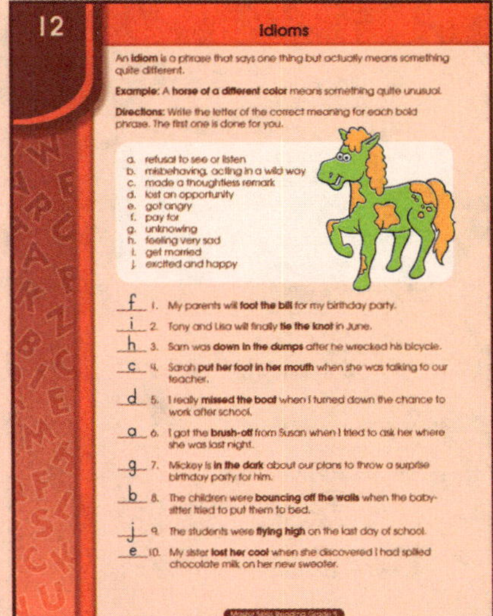

Idioms

An **idiom** is a phrase that says one thing but actually means something quite different.

Example: A **horse of a different color** means something quite unusual.

Directions: Write the letter of the correct meaning for each bold phrase. The first one is done for you.

a. refusal to see or listen
b. misbehaving, acting in a wild way
c. made a thoughtless remark
d. lost an opportunity
e. got angry
f. pay for
g. unknowing
h. feeling very sad
i. get married
j. excited and happy

f 1. My parents will **foot the bill** for my birthday party.
i 2. Tony and Lisa will finally **tie the knot** in June.
h 3. Sam was **down in the dumps** after he wrecked his bicycle.
c 4. Sarah **put her foot in her mouth** when she was talking to our teacher.
d 5. I really **missed the boat** when I turned down the chance to work after school.
a 6. I got the **brush-off** from Susan when I tried to ask her where she was last night.
g 7. Mickey is **in the dark** about our plans to throw a surprise birthday party for him.
b 8. The children were **bouncing off the walls** when the baby-sitter tried to put them to bed.
j 9. The students were **flying high** on the last day of school.
e 10. My sister **lost her cool** when she discovered I had spilled chocolate milk on her new sweater.

12

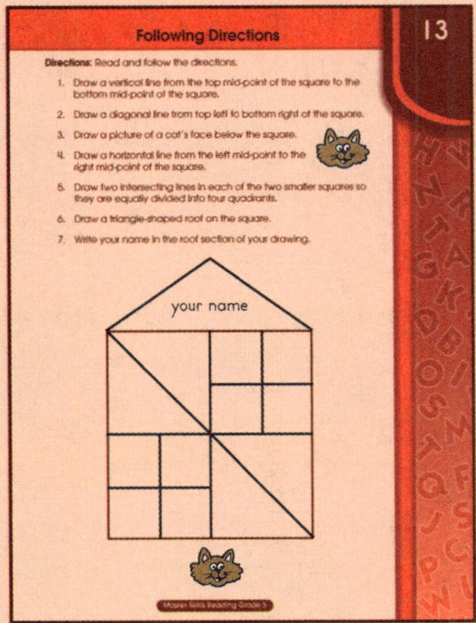

Following Directions

Directions: Read and follow the directions.

1. Draw a vertical line from the top mid-point of the square to the bottom mid-point of the square.
2. Draw a diagonal line from top left to bottom right of the square.
3. Draw a picture of a cat's face below the square.
4. Draw a horizontal line from the left mid-point to the right mid-point of the square.
5. Draw two intersecting lines in each of the two smaller squares so they are equally divided into four quadrants.
6. Draw a triangle-shaped roof on the square.
7. Write your name in the roof section of your drawing.

13

Sequencing

Sequencing *means to place events in order from beginning to end or first to last.*

Example:
To send a letter, you must:
Get paper, pencil or pen, an envelope, and a stamp.
Write the letter.
Fold the letter and put it in the envelope.
Address the envelope correctly.
Put a stamp on the envelope.
Put the envelope in the mailbox or take it to the Post Office.

Directions: Write the sequence for making a peanut butter and jelly sandwich.

Get out bread, peanut butter, jelly, and knife.
Spread jelly on one slice of bread.
Spread peanut butter on the other slice of bread.
Put two pieces of bread together so peanut butter and jelly sides are together.
Put away knife, peanut butter, and jelly.
Enjoy your sandwich.

Directions: After you finish, try making the sandwich **exactly** the way you wrote the steps. Did you leave out any steps? Which ones?

Answers will vary.

Does a particular section you wrote require a better explanation? Clarify your explanation by adding missing information.

14

Answer Key

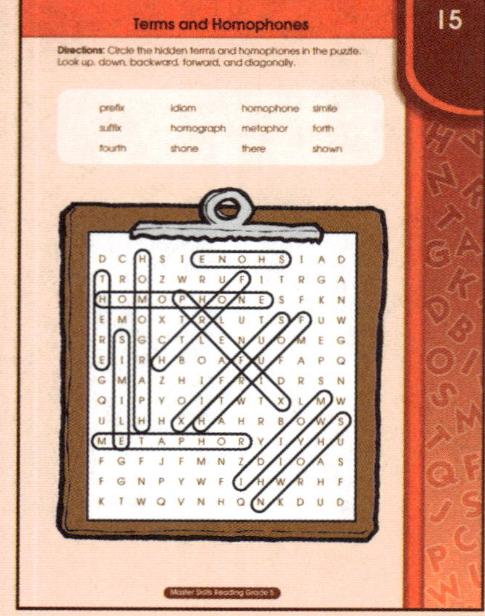

Terms and Homophones

15

Directions: Circle the hidden terms and homophones in the puzzle. Look up, down, backward, forward, and diagonally.

prefix	idiom	homophone	simile
suffix	homograph	metaphor	forth
fourth	shone	there	shown

D C H S I E N O H S I A D
T R O Z W R U F I T R G A
H O M O P H O N E S F K N
E M O X T R L U T S F U W
R S G C T L E N U O M E G
E I R H B O A F U F A P Q
G M A Z H I F R I D R S N
Q I P Y O I T W T X L M W
U L H H X H A H R B O W S
M E T A P H O R Y I Y H U
F G F J F M N Z D I O A S
F G N P Y W F I H W R H F
K T W Q V N H Q N K D U D

Master Skills Reading Grade 5

15

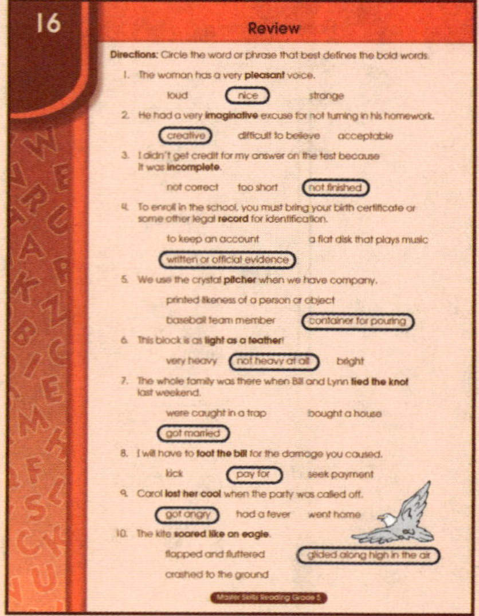

Review

16

Directions: Circle the word or phrase that best defines the bold words.

1. The woman has a very **pleasant** voice.
   loud — nice — strange
2. He had a very **imaginative** excuse for not turning in his homework.
   creative — difficult to believe — acceptable
3. I didn't get credit for my answer on the test because it was **incomplete**.
   not correct — too short — not finished
4. To enroll in the school, you must bring your birth certificate or some other legal **record** for identification.
   to keep an account — a flat disk that plays music — written or official evidence
5. We use the crystal **pitcher** when we have company.
   printed likeness of a person or object — baseball team member — container for pouring
6. This block is as **light as a feather**!
   very heavy — not heavy at all — bright
7. The whole family was there when Bill and Lynn **tied the knot** last weekend.
   were caught in a trap — bought a house — got married
8. I will have to **foot the bill** for the damage you caused.
   kick — pay for — seek payment
9. Carol **lost her cool** when the party was called off.
   got angry — had a fever — went home
10. The kite **soared like an eagle**.
    flapped and fluttered — glided along high in the air — crashed to the ground

Master Skills Reading Grade 5

16

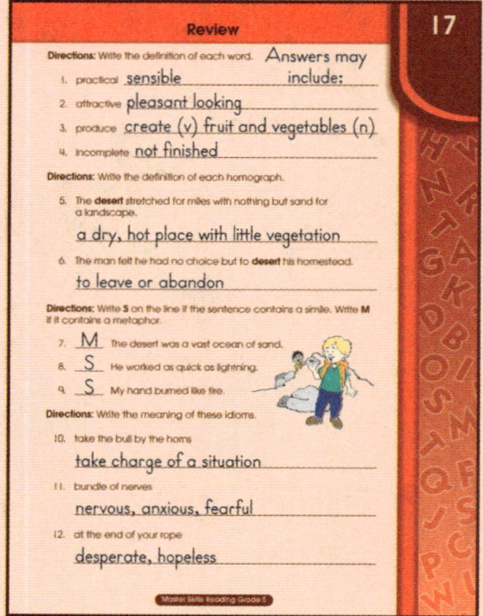

Review

17

Directions: Write the definition of each word. Answers may include:

1. practical sensible
2. attractive pleasant looking
3. produce create (v) fruit and vegetables (n)
4. incomplete not finished

Directions: Write the definition of each homograph.

5. The **desert** stretched for miles with nothing but sand for a landscape.
   a dry, hot place with little vegetation
6. The man felt he had no choice but to **desert** his homestead.
   to leave or abandon

Directions: Write **S** on the line if the sentence contains a simile. Write **M** if it contains a metaphor.

7. M The desert was a vast ocean of sand.
8. S He worked as quick as lightning.
9. S My hand burned like fire.

Directions: Write the meaning of these idioms.

10. take the bull by the horns
    take charge of a situation
11. bundle of nerves
    nervous, anxious, fearful
12. at the end of your rope
    desperate, hopeless

Master Skills Reading Grade 5

17

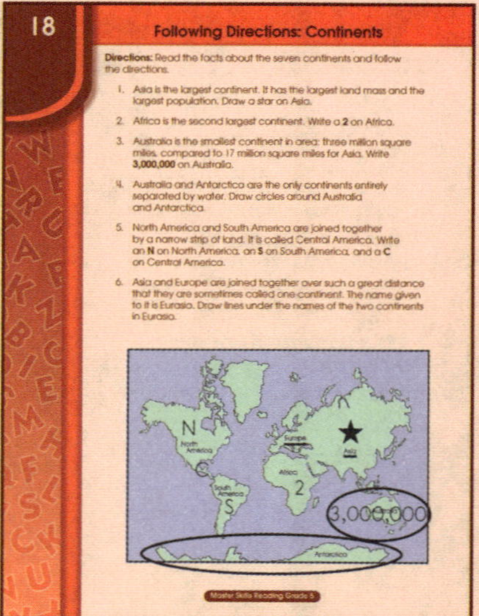

Following Directions: Continents

18

Directions: Read the facts about the seven continents and follow the directions.

1. Asia is the largest continent. It has the largest land mass and the largest population. Draw a star on Asia.
2. Africa is the second largest continent. Write a **2** on Africa.
3. Australia is the smallest continent in area: three million square miles, compared to 17 million square miles for Asia. Write **3,000,000** on Australia.
4. Australia and Antarctica are the only continents entirely separated by water. Draw circles around Australia and Antarctica.
5. North America and South America are joined together by a narrow strip of land. It is called Central America. Write an **N** on North America, an **S** on South America, and a **C** on Central America.
6. Asia and Europe are joined together over such a great distance that they are sometimes called one continent. The name given to it is Eurasia. Draw lines under the names of the two continents in Eurasia.

Master Skills Reading Grade 5

18

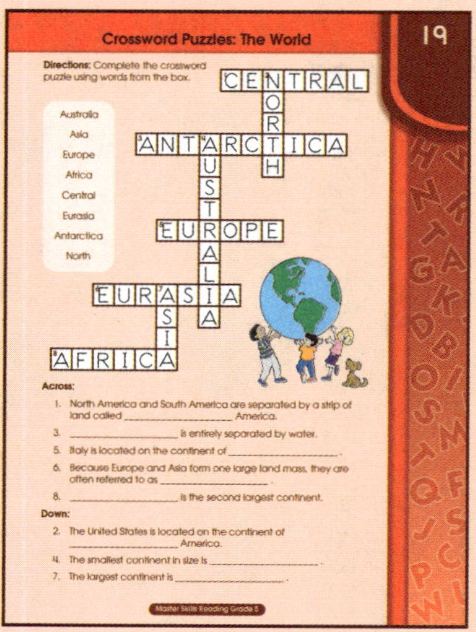

Crossword Puzzles: The World

19

Directions: Complete the crossword puzzle using words from the box.

Australia
Asia
Europe
Africa
Central
Eurasia
Antarctica
North

Across:

1. North America and South America are separated by a strip of land called ________________ America.
3. ________________ is entirely separated by water.
5. Italy is located on the continent of ________________.
6. Because Europe and Asia form one large land mass, they are often referred to as ________________.
8. ________________ is the second largest continent.

Down:

2. The United States is located on the continent of ________________ America.
4. The smallest continent in size is ________________.
7. The largest continent is ________________.

Master Skills Reading Grade 5

19

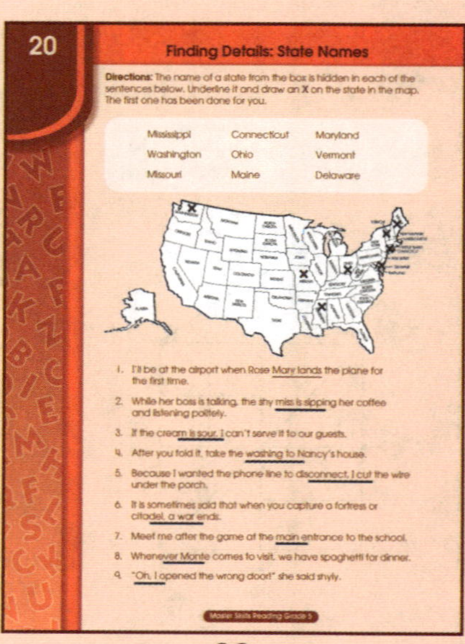

Finding Details: State Names

20

Directions: The name of a state from the box is hidden in each of the sentences below. Underline it and draw an **X** on the state in the map. The first one has been done for you.

Mississippi	Connecticut	Maryland
Washington	Ohio	Vermont
Missouri	Maine	Delaware

1. I'll be at the airport when Rose Mary lands the plane for the first time.
2. While her boss is talking, the shy miss is sipping her coffee and listening politely.
3. If the cream is sour, I can't serve it to our guests.
4. After you fold it, take the washing to Nancy's house.
5. Because I wanted the phone line to disconnect, I cut the wire under the porch.
6. It is sometimes said that when you capture a fortress or citadel, a war ends.
7. Meet me after the game at the main entrance to the school.
8. Whenever Monte comes to visit, we have spaghetti for dinner.
9. "Oh, I opened the wrong door!" she said shyly.

Master Skills Reading Grade 5

20

Answer Key

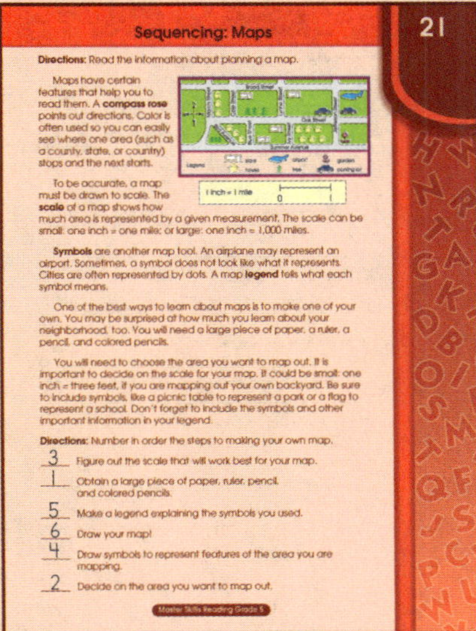

Sequencing: Maps

Directions: Read the information about planning a map.

Maps have certain features that help you to read them. A **compass rose** points out directions. Color is often used so you can easily see where one area (such as a county, state, or country) stops and the next starts.

To be accurate, a map must be drawn to scale. The **scale** of a map shows how much area is represented by a given measurement. The scale can be small: one inch = one mile; or large: one inch = 1,000 miles.

Symbols are another map tool. An airplane may represent an airport. Sometimes, a symbol does not look like what it represents. Cities are often represented by dots. A map **legend** tells what each symbol means.

One of the best ways to learn about maps is to make one of your own. You may be surprised at how much you learn about your neighborhood, too. You will need a large piece of paper, a ruler, a pencil, and colored pencils.

You will need to choose the area you want to map out. It is important to decide on the scale for your map. It could be small: one inch = three feet, if you are mapping out your own backyard. Be sure to include symbols, like a picnic table to represent a park or a flag to represent a school. Don't forget to include the symbols and other important information in your legend.

Directions: Number in order the steps to making your own map.

3 Figure out the scale that will work best for your map.
1 Obtain a large piece of paper, ruler, pencil, and colored pencils.
5 Make a legend explaining the symbols you used.
6 Draw your map!
4 Draw symbols to represent features of the area you are mapping.
2 Decide on the area you want to map out.

Master Skills Reading Grade 5

21

Reading Skills: Maps

Directions: Use this map to answer the questions.

1. What state borders Louisiana to the north?
   Arkansas
2. What is the state capital of Louisiana?
   Baton Rouge
3. In which direction would you be traveling if you drove from Monroe to Alexandria?
   Southwest
4. About how far is it from Alexandria to Lake Charles?
   About 125 miles
5. Besides Arkansas, name one other state that borders Louisiana.
   Texas/Mississippi

Master Skills Reading Grade 5

22

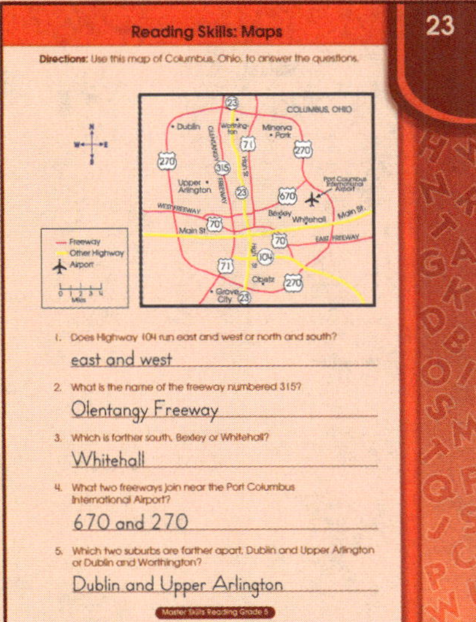

Reading Skills: Maps

Directions: Use this map of Columbus, Ohio, to answer the questions.

1. Does Highway 104 run east and west or north and south?
   east and west
2. What is the name of the freeway numbered 315?
   Olentangy Freeway
3. Which is farther south, Bexley or Whitehall?
   Whitehall
4. What two freeways join near the Port Columbus International Airport?
   670 and 270
5. Which two suburbs are farther apart, Dublin and Upper Arlington or Dublin and Worthington?
   Dublin and Upper Arlington

Master Skills Reading Grade 5

23

Creating a Map

Directions: In the space below, draw a map of your street or town. Be sure to include a compass rose, scale, symbols, and a map legend.

Maps will vary.

Master Skills Reading Grade 5

24

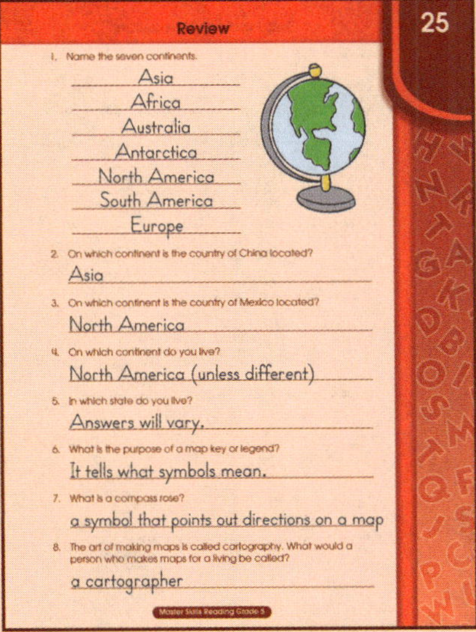

Review

1. Name the seven continents.
   Asia
   Africa
   Australia
   Antarctica
   North America
   South America
   Europe
2. On which continent is the country of China located?
   Asia
3. On which continent is the country of Mexico located?
   North America
4. On which continent do you live?
   North America (unless different)
5. In which state do you live?
   Answers will vary.
6. What is the purpose of a map key or legend?
   It tells what symbols mean.
7. What is a compass rose?
   a symbol that points out directions on a map
8. The art of making maps is called cartography. What would a person who makes maps for a living be called?
   a cartographer

Master Skills Reading Grade 5

25

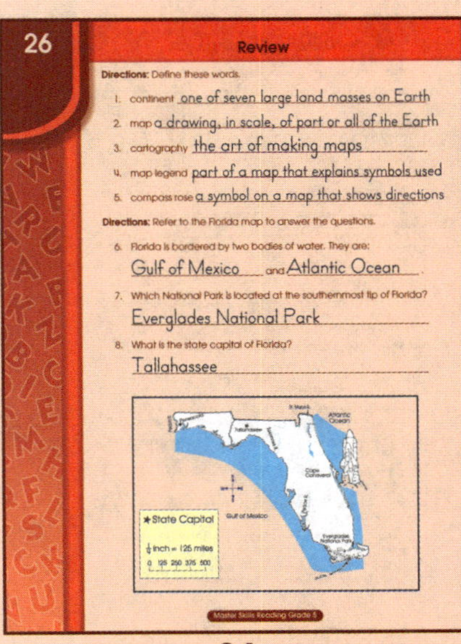

Review

Directions: Define these words.

1. continent one of seven large land masses on Earth
2. map a drawing, in scale, of part or all of the Earth
3. cartography the art of making maps
4. map legend part of a map that explains symbols used
5. compass rose a symbol on a map that shows directions

Directions: Refer to the Florida map to answer the questions.

6. Florida is bordered by two bodies of water. They are:
   Gulf of Mexico and Atlantic Ocean
7. Which National Park is located at the southernmost tip of Florida?
   Everglades National Park
8. What is the state capital of Florida?
   Tallahassee

Master Skills Reading Grade 5

26

Answer Key

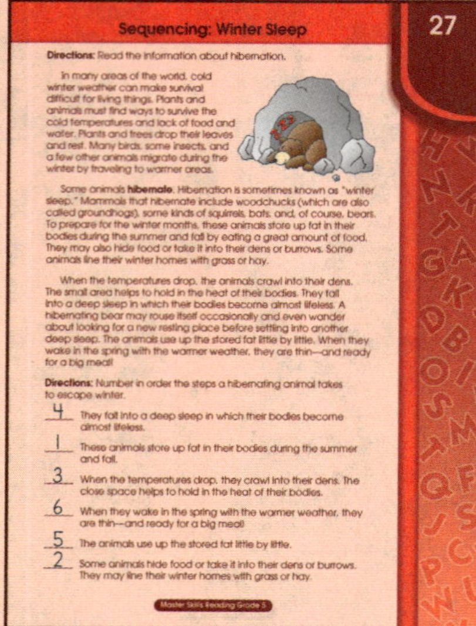

Sequencing: Winter Sleep

27

Directions: Read the information about hibernation.

In many areas of the world, cold winter weather can make survival difficult for living things. Plants and animals must find ways to survive the cold temperatures and lack of food and water. Plants and trees drop their leaves and rest. Many birds, some insects, and a few other animals migrate during the winter by traveling to warmer areas.

Some animals **hibernate**. Hibernation is sometimes known as "winter sleep." Mammals that hibernate include woodchucks (which are also called groundhogs), some kinds of squirrels, bats, and, of course, bears. To prepare for the winter months, these animals store up fat in their bodies during the summer and fall by eating a great amount of food. They may also hide food or take it into their dens or burrows. Some animals line their winter homes with grass or hay.

When the temperatures drop, the animals crawl into their dens. The small area helps to hold in the heat of their bodies. They fall into a deep sleep in which their bodies become almost lifeless. A hibernating bear may rouse itself occasionally and even wander about looking for a new resting place before settling into another deep sleep. The animals use up the stored fat little by little. When they wake in the spring with the warmer weather, they are thin—and ready for a big meal!

Directions: Number in order the steps a hibernating animal takes to escape winter.

4 They fall into a deep sleep in which their bodies become almost lifeless.

1 These animals store up fat in their bodies during the summer and fall.

3 When the temperatures drop, they crawl into their dens. The close space helps to hold in the heat of their bodies.

6 When they wake in the spring with the warmer weather, they are thin—and ready for a big meal!

5 The animals use up the stored fat little by little.

2 Some animals hide food or take it into their dens or burrows. They may line their winter homes with grass or hay.

Master Skills Reading Grade 5

27

Main Idea: Active Winter Animals

28

The **main idea** is the most important point in an article.

Directions: Read the information about animals that are active in winter. Then, answer the questions.

Although many animals hibernate during the cold winter months, there are many animals that stay active. Animals like deer, rabbits, mice, and foxes all remain in their **territory** and hunt during the winter.

These animals must eat a great deal before winter arrives in order to put on an extra layer of fat. This layer of fat is necessary to prevent them from starving when food becomes scarce in the cold weather.

Animals that stay active in the winter also grow thick coats of fur. The heavier coats act as **insulation** against the winds and cold weather and help keep them warm.

Even animals that remain active in winter need warm shelters for protection during winter storms and for sleeping. The shelters may be small holes, blankets of leaves or other **vegetation**, or rock cavities.

Winter is not an easy time for animals, but those with thick coats of fur, sufficient food, a good layer of fat, and warm shelter usually manage to survive.

1. What is the main idea of the selection?
   Animals that remain active in winter need thick fur, lots of food, a layer of fat, and warm shelter to survive.
2. What is necessary for survival in the winter?
   thick fur, food, layer of fat, shelter
3. Define these words. Use a dictionary if needed.
   territory area where an animal lives
   insulation something used to keep out cold
   vegetation plants
4. If you were an animal, would you want to hibernate or stay active? Why?
   Answers will vary.

Master Skills Reading Grade 5

28

Context Clues: Migration

29

Using **context clues** is a way to figure out the meaning of a new word by relating it to the other words in the sentence. This is called learning the meaning from **context**.

Directions: Read the information about migration. Then, write the answers.

For hundreds of years, people believed that the yearly disappearance of some types of birds meant that they hibernated like bears and woodchucks. Today, scientists know that birds **migrate** to warmer climates for the cold winter months.

Even though scientists know that birds migrate, they are still unsure about why and how they migrate. Many birds have two homes—one for winter and one for summer. Every year, these birds travel from one place to the other. North American birds, which depend on fruit, nectar, and insects, travel south for the winter. **Tropical** birds travel north when it is too hot and dry in that area.

Migration is an amazing feat, even though it is difficult to understand and believe. Some birds travel up to 5,000 miles, and many will return to the same yard, pond, or tree each year! Birds are excellent **navigators**, and scientists believe they may use a combination of landmarks, the stars, the sun, and their hearing to help locate their destinations.

Birds also seem to know instinctively when to begin their migration. Some scientists believe that the **instinct** to migrate is aided by chemical changes in the birds' bodies brought about by shorter daylight hours.

Regardless of how or why birds migrate, the simple fact that such small animals can travel thousands of miles to the same speck of land or water is an incredible accomplishment!

1. Define these words as they are used in the article on migration.
   instinct knowledge an animal is born with
   tropical warm climate
   navigator one who finds the way
2. Explain how birds find their homes while migrating.
   They use landmarks, the stars, the sun, and their hearing
3. Birds are born with the instinct to migrate. Name another animal that is born with an instinct and describe it.
   Answers will vary.

Master Skills Reading Grade 5

29

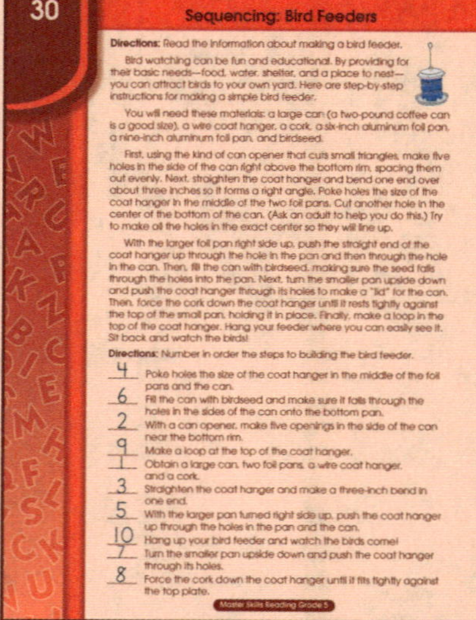

Sequencing: Bird Feeders

30

Directions: Read the information about making a bird feeder.

Bird watching can be fun and educational. By providing for their basic needs—food, water, shelter, and a place to nest—you can attract birds to your own yard. Here are step-by-step instructions for making a simple bird feeder.

You will need these materials: a large can (a two-pound coffee can is a good size), a wire coat hanger, a cork, a six-inch aluminum foil pan, a nine-inch aluminum foil pan, and birdseed.

First, using the kind of can opener that cuts small triangles, make five holes in the side of the can right above the bottom rim, spacing them out evenly. Next, straighten the coat hanger and bend one end over about three inches so it forms a right angle. Poke holes the size of the coat hanger in the middle of the two foil pans. Cut another hole in the center of the bottom of the can. (Ask an adult to help you do this.) Try to make all the holes in the exact center so they will line up.

With the larger foil pan right side up, push the straight end of the coat hanger up through the hole in the pan and then through the hole in the can. Then, fill the can with birdseed, making sure the seed falls through the holes into the pan. Next, turn the smaller pan upside down and push the coat hanger through its holes to make a "lid" for the can. Then, force the cork down the coat hanger until it rests tightly against the top of the small pan, holding it in place. Finally, make a loop in the top of the coat hanger. Hang your feeder where you can easily see it. Sit back and watch the birds!

Directions: Number in order the steps to building the bird feeder.

4 Poke holes the size of the coat hanger in the middle of the foil pans and the can.

6 Fill the can with birdseed and make sure it falls through the holes in the sides of the can onto the bottom pan.

2 With a can opener, make five openings in the side of the can near the bottom rim.

9 Make a loop at the top of the coat hanger.

1 Obtain a large can, two foil pans, a wire coat hanger, and a cork.

3 Straighten the coat hanger and make a three-inch bend in one end.

5 With the larger pan turned right side up, push the coat hanger up through the holes in the pan and the can.

10 Hang up your bird feeder and watch the birds come!

7 Turn the smaller pan upside down and push the coat hanger through its holes.

8 Force the cork down the coat hanger until it fits tightly against the top plate.

Master Skills Reading Grade 5

30

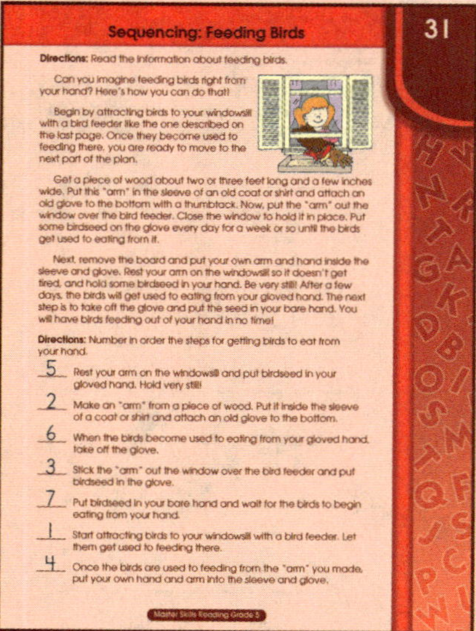

Sequencing: Feeding Birds

31

Directions: Read the information about feeding birds.

Can you imagine feeding birds right from your hand? Here's how you can do that!

Begin by attracting birds to your windowsill with a bird feeder like the one described on the last page. Once they become used to feeding there, you are ready to move to the next part of the plan.

Get a piece of wood about two or three feet long and a few inches wide. Put this "arm" in the sleeve of an old coat or shirt and attach an old glove to the bottom with a thumbtack. Now, put the "arm" out the window over the bird feeder. Close the window to hold it in place. Put some birdseed on the glove every day for a week or so until the birds get used to eating from it.

Next, remove the board and put your own arm and hand inside the sleeve and glove. Rest your arm on the windowsill so it doesn't get tired, and hold some birdseed in your hand. Be very still! After a few days, the birds will get used to eating from your gloved hand. The next step is to take off the glove and put the seed in your bare hand. You will have birds feeding out of your hand in no time!

Directions: Number in order the steps for getting birds to eat from your hand.

5 Rest your arm on the windowsill and put birdseed in your gloved hand. Hold very still!

2 Make an "arm" from a piece of wood. Put it inside the sleeve of a coat or shirt and attach an old glove to the bottom.

6 When the birds become used to eating from your gloved hand, take off the glove.

3 Stick the "arm" out the window over the bird feeder and put birdseed in the glove.

7 Put birdseed in your bare hand and wait for the birds to begin eating from your hand.

1 Start attracting birds to your windowsill with a bird feeder. Let them get used to feeding there.

4 Once the birds are used to feeding from the "arm" you made, put your own hand and arm into the sleeve and glove.

Master Skills Reading Grade 5

31

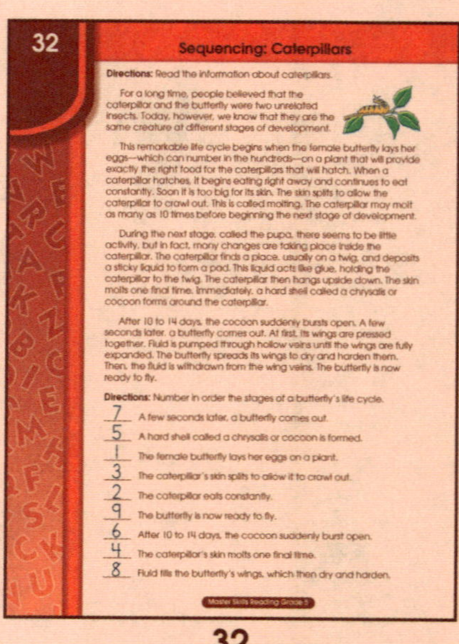

Sequencing: Caterpillars

32

Directions: Read the information about caterpillars.

For a long time, people believed that the caterpillar and the butterfly were two unrelated insects. Today, however, we know that they are the same creature at different stages of development.

This remarkable life cycle begins when the female butterfly lays her eggs—which can number in the hundreds—on a plant that will provide exactly the right food for the caterpillars that will hatch. When a caterpillar hatches, it begins eating right away and continues to eat constantly. Soon it is too big for its skin. The skin splits to allow the caterpillar to crawl out. This is called molting. The caterpillar may molt as many as 10 times before beginning the next stage of development.

During the next stage, called the pupa, there seems to be little activity, but in fact, many changes are taking place inside the caterpillar. The caterpillar finds a place, usually on a twig, and deposits a sticky liquid to form a pad. This liquid acts like glue, holding the caterpillar to the twig. The caterpillar then hangs upside down. The skin molts one final time. Immediately, a hard shell called a chrysalis or cocoon forms around the caterpillar.

After 10 to 14 days, the cocoon suddenly bursts open. A few seconds later, a butterfly comes out. At first, its wings are pressed together. Fluid is pumped through hollow veins until the wings are fully expanded. The butterfly spreads its wings to dry and harden them. Then, the fluid is withdrawn from the wing veins. The butterfly is now ready to fly.

Directions: Number in order the stages of a butterfly's life cycle.

7 A few seconds later, a butterfly comes out.

5 A hard shell called a chrysalis or cocoon is formed.

1 The female butterfly lays her eggs on a plant.

3 The caterpillar's skin splits to allow it to crawl out.

2 The caterpillar eats constantly.

9 The butterfly is now ready to fly.

6 After 10 to 14 days, the cocoon suddenly burst open.

4 The caterpillar's skin molts one final time.

8 Fluid fills the butterfly's wings, which then dry and harden.

Master Skills Reading Grade 5

32

Review

33

Directions: Write the answers.

1. Define hibernation. winter sleep
2. Name an animal that hibernates. Sample answers: bears, bats, etc.
3. Define migration. The process of moving from one location to another.
4. Name an animal that migrates. Answers will vary.
5. Do you have a bird feeder at home? Answers will vary.
6. Why is it important to keep the bird feeder filled with seeds throughout the winter? Answers will vary. Example: so the birds do not starve
7. What four stages of development does a butterfly go through? egg, caterpillar, pupa, (chrysalis), butterfly

Master Skills Reading Grade 5

33

Review

34

Directions: Write the answers.

1. Explain the difference between hibernation and migration. Hibernation means to sleep through the winter. Migration means to go to a warmer climate in the winter.
2. List at least three animals that fit each category.

Hibernates	Migrates
bats	birds
bears	whales
woodchucks	butterflies

3. Consider this problem. A man enjoys feeding birds in his wooded backyard during winter. However, because there are many trees, he also has a large squirrel population. Whenever he fills his bird feeders, they are emptied within minutes by the crafty and gymnastic squirrels.

What can the man do to solve his problem? Explain your solution in paragraph form below.

Answers will vary.

Master Skills Reading Grade 5

34

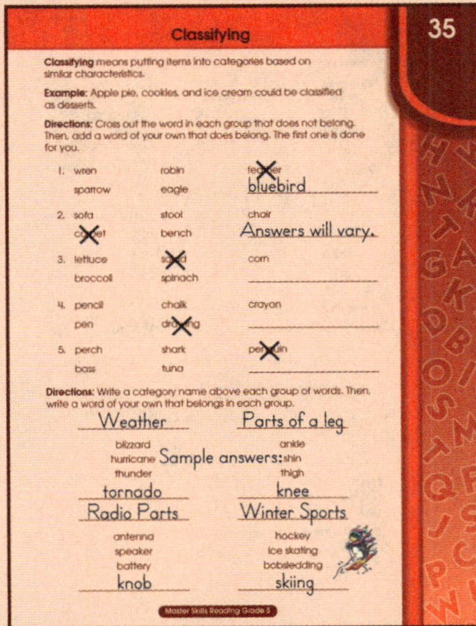

Classifying

35

Classifying means putting items into categories based on similar characteristics.

Example: Apple pie, cookies, and ice cream could be classified as desserts.

Directions: Cross out the word in each group that does not belong. Then, add a word of your own that does belong. The first one is done for you.

1. wren, robin, ~~feather~~, sparrow, eagle — bluebird
2. sofa, stool, chair, ~~closet~~, bench — Answers will vary.
3. lettuce, ~~salad~~, corn, broccoli, spinach
4. pencil, chalk, crayon, pen, ~~drawing~~
5. perch, shark, ~~penguin~~, bass, tuna

Directions: Write a category name above each group of words. Then, write a word of your own that belongs in each group.

Sample answers:

Weather	Parts of a leg
blizzard	ankle
hurricane	shin
thunder	thigh
tornado	knee

Radio Parts	Winter Sports
antenna	hockey
speaker	ice skating
battery	bobsledding
knob	skiing

Master Skills Reading Grade 5

35

Classifying

36

Directions: Write three objects which could belong in each category.

1.	whales	humpback	blue	killer
2.	songs	Happy Birthday	Blue Suede Shoes	Are You Sleeping?
3.	sports stars	Michael Jordan	Stephi Graff	Jeff Gordon
4.	fruit	apple	lemon	banana
5.	schools	Lincoln High	Harvard	UCLA
6.	teachers	Ms. McCall	Mr. Springer	Dr. Burns
7.	tools	hammer	broom	ax
8.	friends	Gabriel	Bailey	Cole
9.	books	Huckleberry Finn	A Wrinkle in Time	Watership Down
10.	mammals	bear	bat	people
11.	fish	bass	cod	shark
12.	desserts	cookies	cake	pie
13.	cars	Ford	Chevy	Volkswagen
14.	hobbies	Collecting Stamps	painting	gardening
15.	vegetables	potatoes	spinach	eggplant

Master Skills Reading Grade 5

36

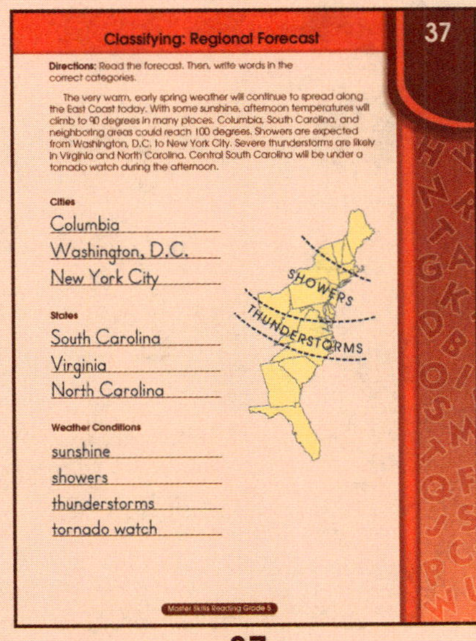

Classifying: Regional Forecast

37

Directions: Read the forecast. Then, write words in the correct categories.

The very warm, early spring weather will continue to spread along the East Coast today. With some sunshine, afternoon temperatures will climb to 90 degrees in many places. Columbia, South Carolina, and neighboring areas could reach 100 degrees. Showers are expected from Washington, D.C. to New York City. Severe thunderstorms are likely in Virginia and North Carolina. Central South Carolina will be under a tornado watch during the afternoon.

Cities

Columbia
Washington, D.C.
New York City

States

South Carolina
Virginia
North Carolina

Weather Conditions

sunshine
showers
thunderstorms
tornado watch

Master Skills Reading Grade 5

37

Analogies

38

An **analogy** is a way of comparing objects to show how they relate.

Example: Nose is to smell as tongue is to taste.

Directions: Write the correct word on the blank to fill in the missing part of each analogy. The first one is done for you.

1. Scissors are to paper as saw is to wood.
   fold (scissors) thin
2. Man is to boy as woman is to girl.
   mother (girl) lady
3. attic is to cellar as sky is to ground.
   down (attic) up
4. Rag is to dust as broom is to sweep.
   floor straw (broom)
5. Freezer is to cold as stove is to hot.
   cook (hot) recipe
6. Car is to garage as book is to bookshelf.
   ride gas (garage)
7. Window is to glass as car is to metal.
   (glass) clear house
8. Eyes are to seeing as feet are to walking.
   legs (walking) shoes
9. Gas is to car as electricity is to lamp.
   (electricity) plug cord
10. Refrigerator is to food as closet is to clothes.
    fold material (closet)
11. Floor is to down as ceiling is to up.
    high over (up)
12. Pillow is to soft as rock is to hard.
    dirt (hard) hurt

Master Skills Reading Grade 5

38

Answer Key

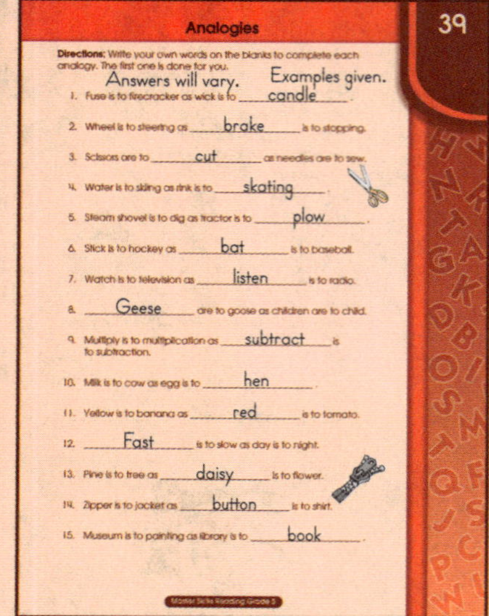

Analogies

39

Directions: Write your own words on the blanks to complete each analogy. The first one is done for you.

Answers will vary. Examples given.

1. Fuse is to firecracker as wick is to candle.
2. Wheel is to steering as brake is to stopping.
3. Scissors are to cut as needles are to sew.
4. Water is to skiing as rink is to skating.
5. Steam shovel is to dig as tractor is to plow.
6. Stick is to hockey as bat is to baseball.
7. Watch is to television as listen is to radio.
8. Geese are to goose as children are to child.
9. Multiply is to multiplication as subtract is to subtraction.
10. Milk is to cow as egg is to hen.
11. Yellow is to banana as red is to tomato.
12. Fast is to slow as day is to night.
13. Pine is to tree as daisy is to flower.
14. Zipper is to jacket as button is to shirt.
15. Museum is to painting as library is to book.

Master Skills Reading Grade 5

39

Facts and Opinions

40

A **fact** is information that can be proved.

Example: Hawaii is a state.

An **opinion** is a belief. It tells what someone thinks. It cannot be proved.

Example: Hawaii is the prettiest state.

Directions: Write **f** (fact) or **o** (opinion) on the line by each sentence. The first one is done for you.

f 1. Hawaii is the only island state.
o 2. The best fishing is in Michigan.
o 3. It is easy to find a job in Wyoming.
f 4. Trenton is the capital of New Jersey.
f 5. Kentucky is nicknamed the Bluegrass State.
o 6. The friendliest people in the United States live in Georgia.
o 7. The cleanest beaches are in California.
o 8. Summers are most beautiful in Arizona.
f 9. Only two percent of North Dakota is forest or woodland.
f 10. The first shots of the Civil War were fired in South Carolina on April 12, 1861.
f 11. The varied geographical features of Washington include mountains, deserts, a rainforest, and a volcano.
f 12. In 1959, Alaska and Hawaii became the 49th and 50th states admitted to the Union.
f 13. Wyandotte Cave, one of the largest caves in the United States, is in Indiana.

Directions: Write one fact and one opinion about your own state.

Fact: Answers will vary.

Opinion:

Master Skills Reading Grade 5

40

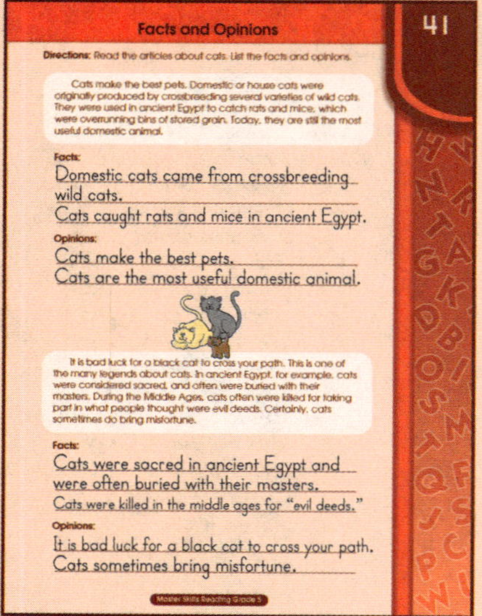

Facts and Opinions

41

Directions: Read the articles about cats. List the facts and opinions.

Cats make the best pets. Domestic or house cats were originally produced by crossbreeding several varieties of wild cats. They were used in ancient Egypt to catch rats and mice, which were overrunning bins of stored grain. Today, they are still the most useful domestic animal.

Facts:
Domestic cats came from crossbreeding wild cats.
Cats caught rats and mice in ancient Egypt.

Opinions:
Cats make the best pets.
Cats are the most useful domestic animal.

It is bad luck for a black cat to cross your path. This is one of the many legends about cats. In ancient Egypt, for example, cats were considered sacred, and often were buried with their masters. During the Middle Ages, cats often were killed for taking part in what people thought were evil deeds. Certainly, cats sometimes do bring misfortune.

Facts:
Cats were sacred in ancient Egypt and were often buried with their masters.
Cats were killed in the middle ages for "evil deeds."

Opinions:
It is bad luck for a black cat to cross your path.
Cats sometimes bring misfortune.

Master Skills Reading Grade 5

41

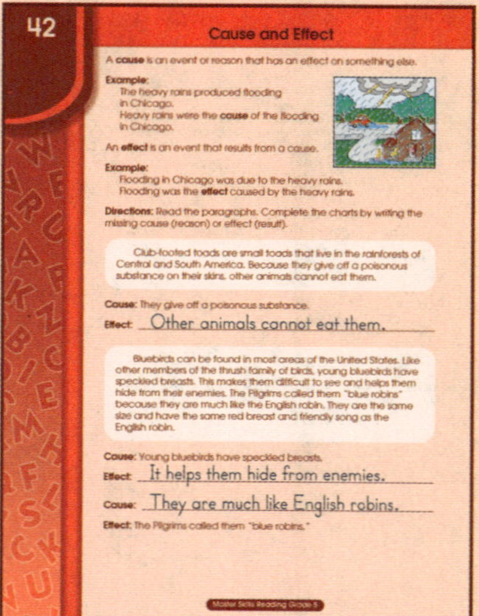

Cause and Effect

42

A **cause** is an event or reason that has an effect on something else.

Example:
The heavy rains produced flooding in Chicago.
Heavy rains were the **cause** of the flooding in Chicago.

An **effect** is an event that results from a cause.

Example:
Flooding in Chicago was due to the heavy rains.
Flooding was the **effect** caused by the heavy rains.

Directions: Read the paragraphs. Complete the charts by writing the missing cause (reason) or effect (result).

Club-footed toads are small toads that live in the rainforests of Central and South America. Because they give off a poisonous substance on their skins, other animals cannot eat them.

Cause: They give off a poisonous substance.
Effect: Other animals cannot eat them.

Bluebirds can be found in most areas of the United States. Like other members of the thrush family of birds, young bluebirds have speckled breasts. This makes them difficult to see and helps them hide from their enemies. The Pilgrims called them "blue robins" because they are much like the English robin. They are the same size and have the same red breast and friendly song as the English robin.

Cause: Young bluebirds have speckled breasts.
Effect: It helps them hide from enemies.
Cause: They are much like English robins.
Effect: The Pilgrims called them "blue robins."

Master Skills Reading Grade 5

42

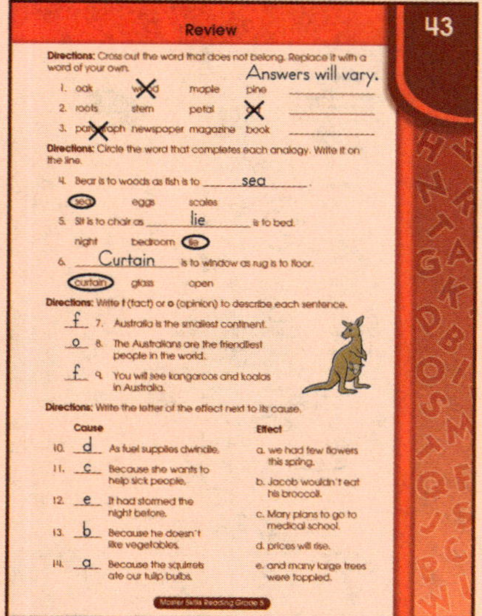

Review

43

Directions: Cross out the word that does not belong. Replace it with a word of your own.

Answers will vary.

1. oak ~~wood~~ maple pine
2. roots stem petal ~~[crossed out]~~
3. ~~paragraph~~ newspaper magazine book

Directions: Circle the word that completes each analogy. Write it on the line.

4. Bear is to woods as fish is to sea.
   (sea) eggs scales
5. Sit is to chair as lie is to bed.
   night bedroom (lie)
6. Curtain is to window as rug is to floor.
   (curtain) glass open

Directions: Write **f** (fact) or **o** (opinion) to describe each sentence.

f 7. Australia is the smallest continent.
o 8. The Australians are the friendliest people in the world.
f 9. You will see kangaroos and koalas in Australia.

Directions: Write the letter of the effect next to its cause.

	Cause	Effect
10. d	As fuel supplies dwindle,	a. we had few flowers this spring.
11. c	Because she wants to help sick people,	b. Jacob wouldn't eat his broccoli.
12. e	It had stormed the night before,	c. Mary plans to go to medical school.
13. b	Because he doesn't like vegetables,	d. prices will rise.
14. a	Because the squirrels ate our tulip bulbs,	e. and many large trees were toppled.

Master Skills Reading Grade 5

43

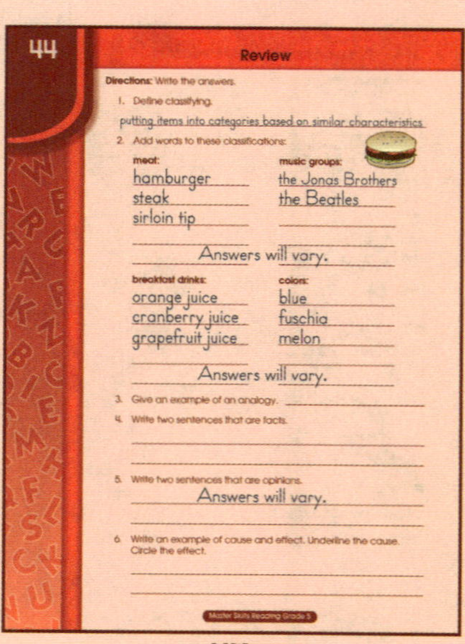

Review

44

Directions: Write the answers.

1. Define classifying.
   putting items into categories based on similar characteristics
2. Add words to these classifications:

meat:	music groups:
hamburger	the Jonas Brothers
steak	the Beatles
sirloin tip	
Answers will vary.	

breakfast drinks:	colors:
orange juice	blue
cranberry juice	fuschia
grapefruit juice	melon
Answers will vary.	

3. Give an example of an analogy.
4. Write two sentences that are facts.
5. Write two sentences that are opinions.
   Answers will vary.
6. Write an example of cause and effect. Underline the cause. Circle the effect.

Master Skills Reading Grade 5

44

Answer Key

45 — Review

Directions: Write a category name for each group.

1. blue jay robin chickadee **birds**
2. baseball soccer football **sports**
3. cumulus cirrus stratus **clouds**
4. Orion Cassiopeia Big Dipper **constellations**
5. humpback blue killer **whales**

Directions: Complete these analogies.

6. Engine is to car as heart is to **body**.
7. Yellow is to banana as red is to **apple**.
8. Photo is to camera as **video** is to camcorder.

Directions: Write two facts and two opinions about a sport.

Facts:

9. ______
10. ______

Opinions: Answers will vary.

11. ______
12. ______

Directions: Complete these sentences with an effect.

13. She enjoyed the book so she ______.
14. Because my teacher is absent, ______.
15. My mom likes broccoli so ______.

Master Skills Reading Grade 5

45

46 — Reading Comprehension: Printing

Directions: Read the information about printing. Then, answer the questions.

When people talk about printing, they usually mean making exact copies of an original document, such as a newspaper, magazine, or an entire book. The inventions that have allowed us to do this are some of the most important developments in history. Look around you at the many examples of printed materials. Can you imagine life without them?

Until the thirteenth century, all material had to be printed by hand, one copy at a time. To make a copy of a book took much time and effort.

The oldest known example of a printed book was made in China in 848 A.D. by Wang Chieh, who carved each page of a book by hand onto a block of wood. He then put ink on the wood and pressed it on paper. The idea of printing with wood blocks spread to Europe.

In about 1440, the German goldsmith Johann Gutenberg developed the idea of movable type. He invented separate letters made of metal for printing. The letters could be joined together to make words and sentences. Ink was applied to the letters to print many copies of the same material. Because they were made of metal, the letters could be used over and over. This wonderful invention made it possible to have more printed material at a lower cost.

Gutenberg had other ideas that were important to printing. He developed a special type of ink that would stick to the new metal letters. Gutenberg's ideas were so successful that the process of printing went almost unchanged for more than 300 years.

1. In what country was the oldest known printed book made?
   China
2. Who made the first printed book?
   Wang Chieh
3. What is movable type?
   separate letters made of metal for printing
4. Who developed the idea of movable type?
   Johann Gutenberg
5. What was another important invention of Gutenberg?
   special ink

Master Skills Reading Grade 5

46

47 — Reading Comprehension: Newspapers

Directions: Read the information about newspapers. Then, answer the questions.

Newspapers keep us informed about what is going on in the world. They entertain, educate, and examine the events of the day. For millions of people worldwide, newspapers are an important part of daily life.

Newspapers are published at various intervals, but they usually come out daily or weekly. Of the nearly 60,000 newspapers published around the world, about 2,600 are published in the United States. More than half—about 1,800—of them are dailies.

Some newspapers have many subscribers—people who pay to have each edition delivered to them. *The Wall Street Journal* and *USA Today* each have about two million subscribers. There are many, many newspapers with only a few thousand subscribers. These include small-town weeklies and special-interest papers, like those written for people who enjoy the same hobby.

Newspapers provide a service to the community by providing information at little cost. But newspaper publishing is a business, so like other businesses, newspapers need to make money. They can keep the cost to subscribers low and still stay in business by selling space to businesses and individuals who want to advertise products or services. In most newspapers, between one-third and two-thirds of the paper is taken up by advertising.

1. About how many newspapers are published worldwide?
   nearly 60,000
2. What services do newspapers provide?
   entertain, educate, examine events
3. What are subscribers?
   people who pay to have newspapers delivered to them
4. How often are most newspapers published?
   daily
5. What do newspapers do to keep the cost to the reader low, but still make money?
   They sell space for ads.
6. In most newspapers, about how much of the paper is taken up by advertising?
   between one-third and two-thirds

Master Skills Reading Grade 5

47

48 — Reading Comprehension: Newspapers

Directions: Read the information about the first newspapers. Then, answer the questions.

Long ago, town criers walked through cities reading important news to the people. The earliest newspapers were probably handwritten notices posted in towns for the public to read.

The first true newspaper was a weekly paper started in Germany in 1609. It was called *The Strassburg Relation*. The Germans were pioneers in newspaper publishing. Johann Gutenberg, the man who developed movable type, was German.

One of the first English-language newspapers, *The London Gazette*, was first printed in England in 1665. Gazette is an old English word that means *official publication*. Many newspapers today still use the word gazette in their names.

In America, several papers began during colonial days. The first successful one, *The Boston News-Letter*, began printing in 1704. It was very small—about the size of a sheet of notebook paper with printing on both sides.

An important date in newspaper publishing was 1833. In that year, *The New York Sun* became the first penny newspaper. The paper actually did cost only a penny. The penny newspapers were similar to today's papers: they printed news while it was still new, they were the first to print advertisements and to sell papers in newsstands, and they were the first to be delivered to homes.

1. How were the earliest newspapers different from today's newspapers?
   They were handwritten notices posted in town.
2. In what year and where was the first true newspaper printed?
   1609 in Germany
3. What was the name of the first successful newspaper in America?
   The Strasburg Relation
4. List four ways penny newspapers were like the newspapers of today.
   printed fresh news
   printed advertisements
   sold at newsstands
   delivered to homes

Master Skills Reading Grade 5

48

49 — Reading Comprehension: Newspaper Jobs

Directions: Read the information about jobs at a newspaper. Then, answer the questions.

It takes an army of people to put out one of the big daily newspapers. Three separate departments are needed to make a newspaper operate smoothly: editorial, mechanical, and business.

The editorial department is the one most people think about first. That is the news-gathering part of the newspaper. The most familiar job in this department is that of the reporter—the person who obtains information for a story and writes it. A photographer takes pictures to go along with the reporter's story.

Editors are the decision-makers. There are many editors at a large newspaper. They assign stories to reporters, read the stories to be certain they are correct, and decide where and if the stories should appearin the paper. The most important stories go on the front page. There are also photo editors who choose which pictures will appear in the paper. Other workers in the editorial department include artists, copy editors, proofreaders, and cartoonists.

The biggest job in the mechanical department is printing the paper. Most large newspapers have their own printing presses. Some small papers send their work to outside printing shops. After an issue, or edition, is printed, it is ready to be sold or "circulated" to the public.

Circulation of the paper is one of the jobs of the business department. This department also sells advertising space. This is very important for newspapers. Many papers make more money selling advertising space than selling newspapers. The business department also takes care of normal business jobs, like paying employees, paying bills, and keeping records.

1. What are the three main departments at a newspaper?
   editorial, mechanical, business
2. Who gets the information for a story and writes it?
   reporter
3. Who are the decision-makers at a newspaper?
   editors
4. What is the biggest job for the mechanical department?
   printing the paper
5. What is the most important job of the business department?
   selling advertising space

Master Skills Reading Grade 5

49

50 — Reading Comprehension: News Stories

Directions: Read the information about news stories. Then, draw a ✓ in the box to show the correct meaning of the bold word.

Here is an example of how a story gets into the newspaper.

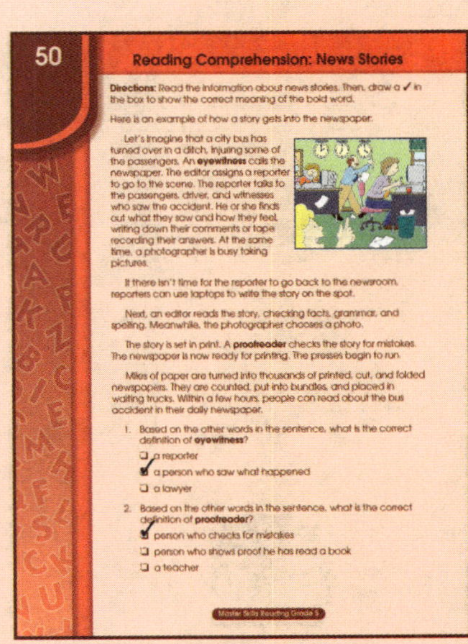

Let's imagine that a city bus has turned over in a ditch, injuring some of the passengers. An **eyewitness** calls the newspaper. The editor assigns a reporter to go to the scene. The reporter talks to the passengers, driver, and witnesses who saw the accident. He or she finds out what they saw and how they feel, writing down their comments or tape recording their answers. At the same time, a photographer is busy taking pictures.

If there isn't time for the reporter to go back to the newsroom, reporters can use laptops to write the story on the spot.

Next, an editor reads the story, checking facts, grammar, and spelling. Meanwhile, the photographer chooses a photo.

The story is set in print. A **proofreader** checks the story for mistakes. The newspaper is now ready for printing. The presses begin to run.

Miles of paper are turned into thousands of printed, cut, and folded newspapers. They are counted, put into bundles, and placed in waiting trucks. Within a few hours, people can read about the bus accident in their daily newspaper.

1. Based on the other words in the sentence, what is the correct definition of **eyewitness**?
   - ☐ a reporter
   - ☑ a person who saw what happened
   - ☐ a lawyer
2. Based on the other words in the sentence, what is the correct definition of **proofreader**?
   - ☑ person who checks for mistakes
   - ☐ person who shows proof he has read a book
   - ☐ a teacher

Master Skills Reading Grade 5

50

Answer Key

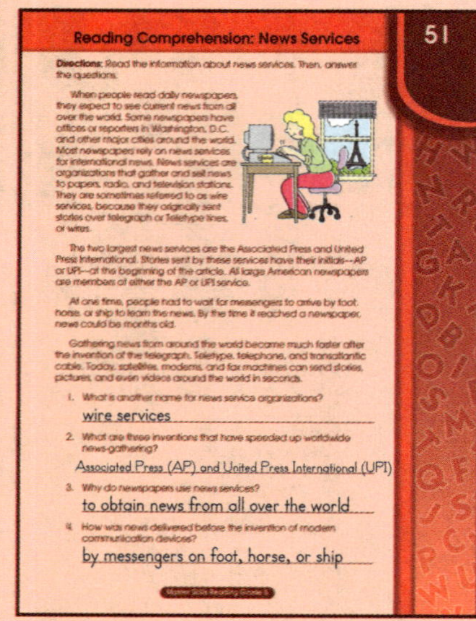

Reading Comprehension: News Services

51

Directions: Read the information about news services. Then, answer the questions.

When people read daily newspapers, they expect to see current news from all over the world. Some newspapers have offices or reporters in Washington, D.C. and other major cities around the world. Most newspapers rely on news services for international news. News services are organizations that gather and sell news to papers, radio, and television stations. They are sometimes referred to as wire services, because they originally sent stories over telegraph or Teletype lines, or wires.

The two largest news services are the Associated Press and United Press International. Stories sent by these services have their initials—AP or UPI—at the beginning of the article. All large American newspapers are members of either the AP or UPI service.

At one time, people had to wait for messengers to arrive by foot, horse, or ship to learn the news. By the time it reached a newspaper, news could be months old.

Gathering news from around the world became much faster after the invention of the telegraph, Teletype, telephone, and transatlantic cable. Today, satellites, modems, and fax machines can send stories, pictures, and even videos around the world in seconds.

1. What is another name for news service organizations?
   wire services
2. What are three inventions that have speeded up worldwide news-gathering?
   Associated Press (AP) and United Press International (UPI)
3. Why do newspapers use news services?
   to obtain news from all over the world
4. How was news delivered before the invention of modern communication devices?
   by messengers on foot, horse, or ship

Master Skills Reading Grade 5

51

Reading Comprehension: Samuel Clemens

52

Directions: Read the information about Samuel Clemens.

Samuel Langhorne Clemens was born in Florida, Missouri, in 1835. In his lifetime, he gained worldwide fame as a writer, lecturer, and humorist.

Clemens first worked for a printer when he was only 12 years old. Soon after that, he worked on his brother's newspaper.

Clemens traveled frequently and worked as a printer in New York, Philadelphia, St. Louis, and Cincinnati. On a trip to New Orleans in 1857, he learned the difficult art of steamboat **piloting**. Clemens loved piloting and later used it as a background for some of his books, including *Life on the Mississippi*.

A few years later, Clemens went to Nevada with his brother and tried gold mining. When this proved unsuccessful, he went back to writing for newspapers. At first, he signed his humorous pieces Josh. In 1863, he began signing them Mark Twain. The words "mark twain" were used by riverboat pilots to mean *two fathoms (12 feet) deep*, water deep enough for steamboats. From then on, Clemens used this now-famous **pseudonym** for all his writing.

As Mark Twain, he received attention from readers all over the world. His best-known works include *Tom Sawyer* and *The Adventures of Huckleberry Finn*. These two books about boyhood adventures remain popular with readers of all ages.

Directions: Check the correct answer.

1. Based on the other words in the sentence, what is the correct definition of **pseudonym**?
   - ☐ book title
   - ☑ a made-up name used by an author
   - ☐ a humorous article
2. Based on the other words in the sentence, what is the correct definition of **piloting**?
   - ☐ driving an airplane
   - ☑ steering a steamboat on a river
   - ☐ being a train engineer

Master Skills Reading Grade 5

52

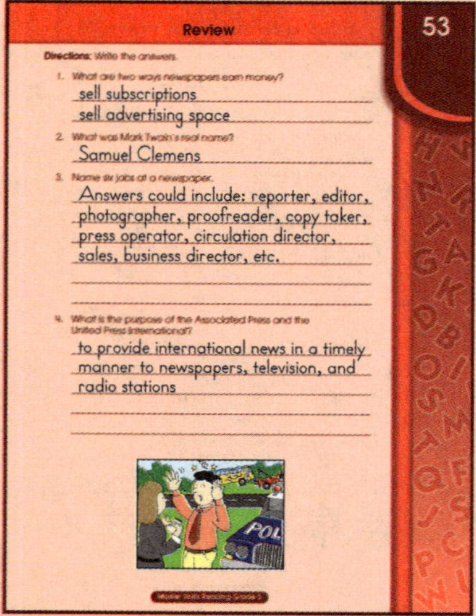

Review

53

Directions: Write the answers.

1. What are two ways newspapers earn money?
   sell subscriptions
   sell advertising space
2. What was Mark Twain's real name?
   Samuel Clemens
3. Name six jobs at a newspaper.
   Answers could include: reporter, editor, photographer, proofreader, copy taker, press operator, circulation director, sales, business director, etc.
4. What is the purpose of the Associated Press and the United Press International?
   to provide international news in a timely manner to newspapers, television, and radio stations

Master Skills Reading Grade 5

53

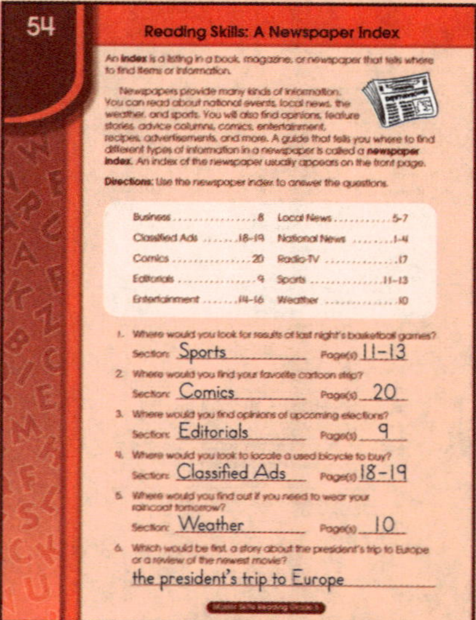

Reading Skills: A Newspaper Index

54

An **index** is a listing in a book, magazine, or newspaper that tells where to find items or information.

Newspapers provide many kinds of information. You can read about national events, local news, the weather, and sports. You will also find opinions, feature stories, advice columns, comics, entertainment, recipes, advertisements, and more. A guide that tells you where to find different types of information in a newspaper is called a **newspaper index**. An index of the newspaper usually appears on the front page.

Directions: Use the newspaper index to answer the questions.

Business 8
Classified Ads 18–19
Comics 20
Editorials 9
Entertainment 14–16
Local News 5–7
National News 1–4
Radio-TV 17
Sports 11–13
Weather 10

1. Where would you look for results of last night's basketball games?
   Section: Sports Page(s) 11–13
2. Where would you find your favorite cartoon strip?
   Section: Comics Page(s) 20
3. Where would you find opinions of upcoming elections?
   Section: Editorials Page(s) 9
4. Where would you look to locate a used bicycle to buy?
   Section: Classified Ads Page(s) 18–19
5. Where would you find out if you need to wear your raincoat tomorrow?
   Section: Weather Page(s) 10
6. Which would be first, a story about the president's trip to Europe or a review of the newest movie?
   the president's trip to Europe

Master Skills Reading Grade 5

54

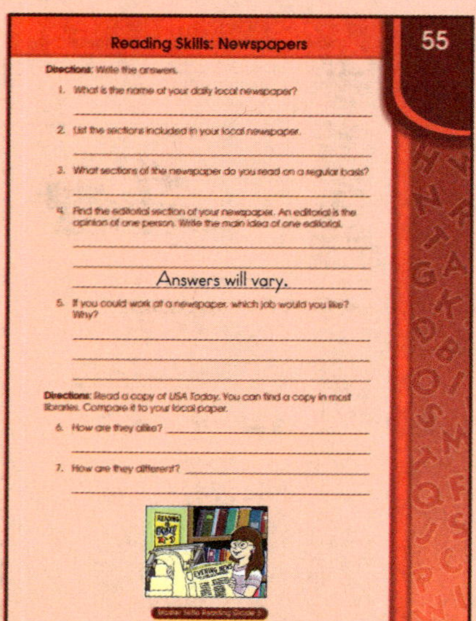

Reading Skills: Newspapers

55

Directions: Write the answers.

1. What is the name of your daily local newspaper?
2. List the sections included in your local newspaper.
3. What sections of the newspaper do you read on a regular basis?
4. Find the editorial section of your newspaper. An editorial is the opinion of one person. Write the main idea of one editorial.
   Answers will vary.
5. If you could work at a newspaper, which job would you like? Why?

Directions: Read a copy of *USA Today*. You can find a copy in most libraries. Compare it to your local paper.

6. How are they alike?
7. How are they different?

Master Skills Reading Grade 5

55

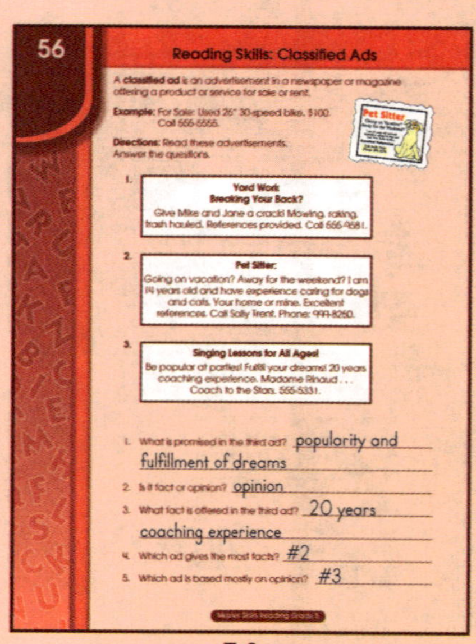

Reading Skills: Classified Ads

56

A **classified ad** is an advertisement in a newspaper or magazine offering a product or service for sale or rent.

Example: For Sale: Used 26" 30-speed bike. $100. Call 555-5555.

Directions: Read these advertisements. Answer the questions.

1. **Yard Work**
   Breaking Your Back?
   Give Mike and Jane a crack! Mowing, raking, trash hauled. References provided. Call 555-9681.
2. **Pet Sitter:**
   Going on vacation? Away for the weekend? I am 14 years old and have experience caring for dogs and cats. Your home or mine. Excellent references. Call Sally Trent. Phone: 999-8250.
3. **Singing Lessons for All Ages!**
   Be popular at parties! Fulfill your dreams! 20 years coaching experience. Madame Rinaud . . . Coach to the Stars. 555-5331.

1. What is promised in the third ad? popularity and fulfillment of dreams
2. Is it fact or opinion? opinion
3. What fact is offered in the third ad? 20 years coaching experience
4. Which ad gives the most facts? #2
5. Which ad is based mostly on opinion? #3

Master Skills Reading Grade 5

56

Answer Key

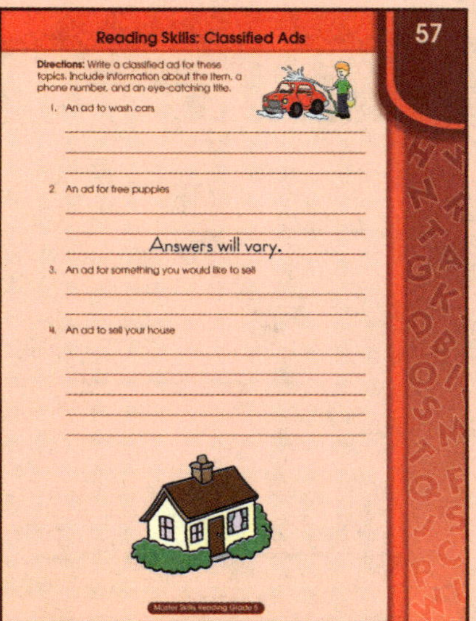

Reading Skills: Classified Ads

Directions: Write a classified ad for these topics. Include information about the item, a phone number, and an eye-catching title.

1. An ad to wash cars
2. An ad for free puppies

Answers will vary.

3. An ad for something you would like to sell
4. An ad to sell your house

Master Skills Reading Grade 5

57

Reading Skills: Schedules

A **schedule** lists events or programs by time, date, and place or channel.

Directions: Use this newspaper television schedule to answer the questions.

Evening

6:00 Let's Talk! Guest: Animal expert Jim Porter
Cartoons
News
News
7:00 Farm Report
Movie. *A Laugh a Minute* (1955) James Rayburn. Comedy about a boy who wants to join the circus.
Spin for Dollars!
Cooking with Cathy. Tonight: Chicken with mushrooms
7:30 Double Trouble (comedy). The twins disrupt the high school dance.
Wall Street Today: Stock Market Report
8:00 NBA Basketball. Teams to be announced.
News Special. "Saving Our Waterways: Pollution in the Mississippi."
Movie. *At Day's End* (1981). Michael Collier, Julie Romer. Drama set in World War II.

1. What two stations have the news at 6:00? 8 and 9
2. What time would you turn on the television to watch a funny movie? 7:00 P.M. What channel? 5
3. What could you watch if you are a sports fan? NBA Basketball
What time and channel is it on? 8:00 P.M. Channel 3
4. Which show title sounds like it could be a game show? Spin for Dollars!

Master Skills Reading Grade 5

58

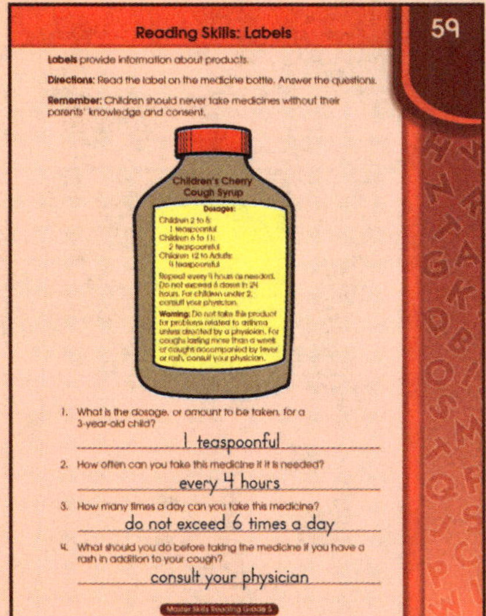

Reading Skills: Labels

Labels provide information about products.

Directions: Read the label on the medicine bottle. Answer the questions.

Remember: Children should never take medicines without their parents' knowledge and consent.

1. What is the dosage, or amount to be taken, for a 3-year-old child? 1 teaspoonful
2. How often can you take this medicine if it is needed? every 4 hours
3. How many times a day can you take this medicine? do not exceed 6 times a day
4. What should you do before taking the medicine if you have a rash in addition to your cough? consult your physician

Master Skills Reading Grade 5

59

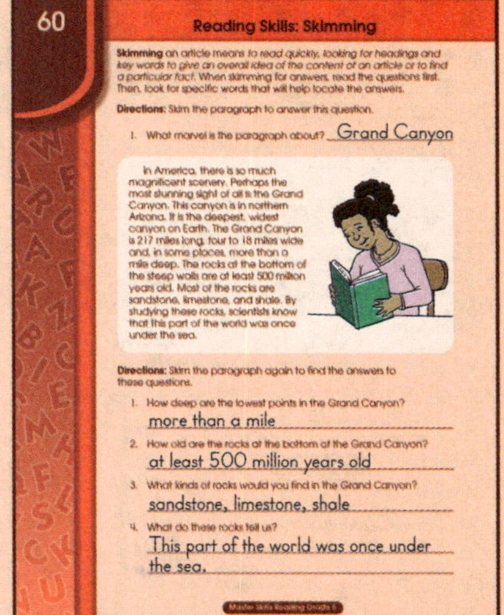

Reading Skills: Skimming

Skimming an article means *to read quickly, looking for headings and key words to give an overall idea of the content of an article or to find a particular fact.* When skimming for answers, read the questions first. Then, look for specific words that will help locate the answers.

Directions: Skim the paragraph to answer this question.

1. What marvel is the paragraph about? Grand Canyon

In America, there is so much magnificent scenery. Perhaps the most stunning sight of all is the Grand Canyon. This canyon is in northern Arizona. It is the deepest, widest canyon on Earth. The Grand Canyon is 217 miles long, four to 18 miles wide and, in some places, more than a mile deep. The rocks at the bottom of the steep walls are at least 500 million years old. Most of the rocks are sandstone, limestone, and shale. By studying these rocks, scientists know that this part of the world was once under the sea.

Directions: Skim the paragraph again to find the answers to these questions.

1. How deep are the lowest points in the Grand Canyon? more than a mile
2. How old are the rocks at the bottom of the Grand Canyon? at least 500 million years old
3. What kinds of rocks would you find in the Grand Canyon? sandstone, limestone, shale
4. What do these rocks tell us? This part of the world was once under the sea.

Master Skills Reading Grade 5

60

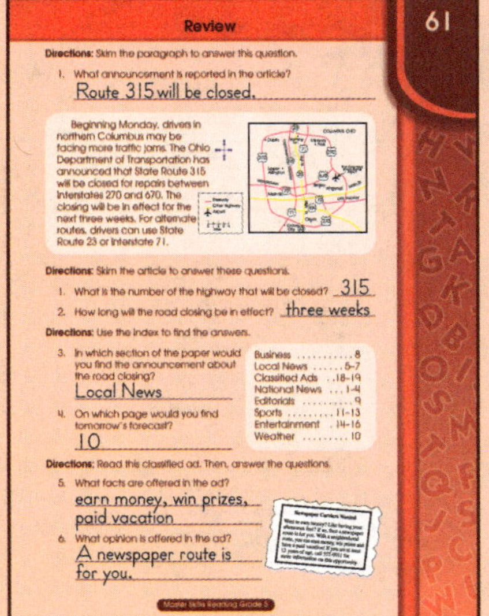

Review

Directions: Skim the paragraph to answer this question.

1. What announcement is reported in the article? Route 315 will be closed.

Beginning Monday, drivers in northern Columbus may be facing more traffic jams. The Ohio Department of Transportation has announced that State Route 315 will be closed for repairs between Interstates 270 and 670. The closing will be in effect for the next three weeks. For alternate routes, drivers can use State Route 23 or Interstate 71.

Directions: Skim the article to answer these questions.

1. What is the number of the highway that will be closed? 315
2. How long will the road closing be in effect? three weeks

Directions: Use the index to find the answers.

3. In which section of the paper would you find the announcement about the road closing? Local News
4. On which page would you find tomorrow's forecast? 10

Business	8
Local News	5-7
Classified Ads	18-19
National News	1-4
Editorials	9
Sports	11-13
Entertainment	14-16
Weather	10

Directions: Read this classified ad. Then, answer the questions.

5. What facts are offered in the ad? earn money, win prizes, paid vacation
6. What opinion is offered in the ad? A newspaper route is for you.

Master Skills Reading Grade 5

61

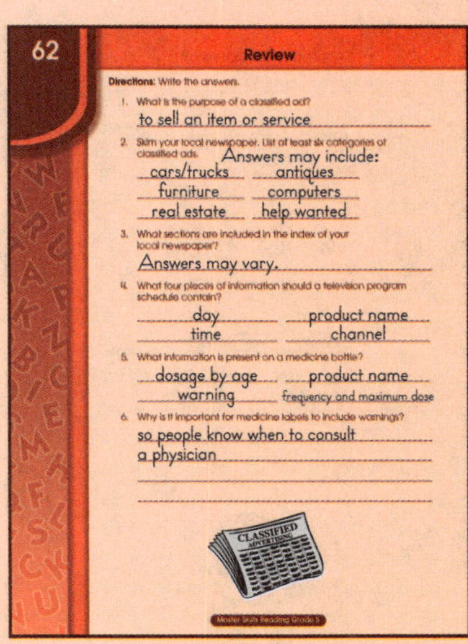

Review

Directions: Write the answers.

1. What is the purpose of a classified ad? to sell an item or service
2. Skim your local newspaper. List at least six categories of classified ads. Answers may include: cars/trucks, antiques, furniture, computers, real estate, help wanted
3. What sections are included in the index of your local newspaper? Answers may vary.
4. What four pieces of information should a television program schedule contain? day, product name, time, channel
5. What information is present on a medicine bottle? dosage by age, product name, warning, frequency and maximum dose
6. Why is it important for medicine labels to include warnings? so people know when to consult a physician

Master Skills Reading Grade 5

62

Answer Key

Recognizing Details: The Coldest Continent

63

Directions: Read the information about Antarctica. Then, answer the questions.

Antarctica lies at the South Pole and is the coldest continent. It is without sunlight for months at a time. Even when the sun does shine, its angle is so slanted that the land receives little warmth. Temperatures often drop to 100 degrees below zero, and a fierce wind blows almost endlessly. Most of the land is covered by snow heaped thousands of feet deep. The snow is so heavy and tightly packed that it forms a great ice cap covering more than 95 percent of the continent.

Considering the conditions, it is no wonder there are no towns or cities in Antarctica. There is no permanent population at all, only small scientific research stations. Many teams of explorers and scientists have braved the freezing cold since Antarctica was sighted in 1820. Some have died in their effort, but a great deal of information has been learned about the continent.

From fossils, pieces of coal, and bone samples, we know that Antarctica was not always an ice-covered land. Scientists believe that 200 million years ago it was connected to southern Africa, South America, Australia, and India. Forests grew in warm swamps, and insects and reptiles thrived there. Today, there are animals that live in and around the waters that border the continent. In fact, the waters surrounding Antarctica contain more life than oceans in warmer areas of the world.

1. Where is Antarctica?
   at the South Pole
2. How much of the continent is covered by an ice cap?
   more than 95 percent
3. When was Antarctica first sighted by explorers?
   1820
4. What clues indicate that Antarctica was not always an ice-covered land?
   fossils, pieces of coal, bone samples

63

Reading Comprehension: The Arctic Circle

64

Directions: Read the article about the Arctic Circle. Then, answer the questions.

On the other side of the globe from Antarctica, at the northernmost part of Earth, is another icy land. This is the Arctic Circle. It includes the North Pole itself and the northern fringes of three continents—Europe, Asia, and North America, including the state of Alaska—as well as Greenland and other islands.

The seasons are opposite at the two ends of Earth. When it is summer in Antarctica, it is winter in the Arctic Circle. In both places, there are very long periods of sunlight in summer and very long nights in the winter. On the poles themselves, there are six full months of sunlight and six full months of darkness each year.

Compared to Antarctica, the summers are surprisingly mild in some areas of the Arctic Circle. Much of the snow cover may melt, and temperatures often reach 50 degrees in July. Antarctica is covered by water—frozen water, of course—so nothing can grow there. Plant growth is limited in the polar regions not only by the cold, but also by wind, lack of water, and the long winter darkness.

In the far north, willow trees grow but only become a few inches high! The annual rings, the circles within the trunk of a tree that show its age and how fast it grows, are so narrow that you need a microscope to see them.

A permanently frozen layer of soil, called **permafrost**, keeps roots from growing deep enough into the ground to anchor a plant. Even if a plant could survive the cold temperatures, it could not grow roots deep enough or strong enough to allow the plant to get very big.

1. What three continents have land included in the Arctic Circle?
   Europe
   Asia
   North America
2. Is the Arctic Circle generally warmer or colder than Antarctica?
   warmer
3. What is **permafrost**? a permanently frozen layer of soil

64

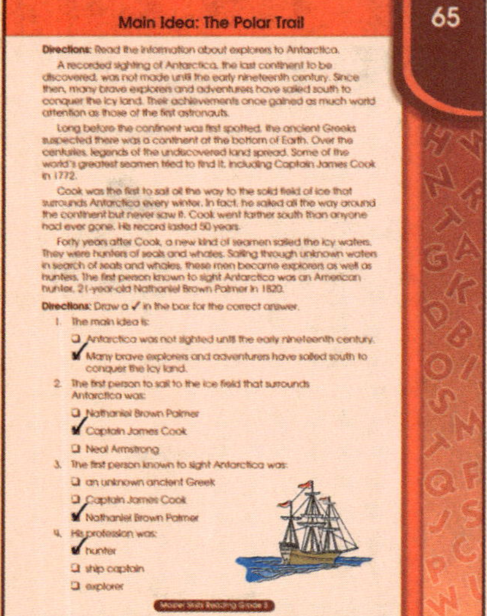

Main Idea: The Polar Trail

65

Directions: Read the information about explorers to Antarctica.

A recorded sighting of Antarctica, the last continent to be discovered, was not made until the early nineteenth century. Since then, many brave explorers and adventures have sailed south to conquer the icy land. Their achievements once gained as much world attention as those of the first astronauts.

Long before the continent was first spotted, the ancient Greeks suspected there was a continent at the bottom of Earth. Over the centuries, legends of the undiscovered land spread. Some of the world's greatest seamen tried to find it, including Captain James Cook in 1772.

Cook was the first to sail all the way to the solid field of ice that surrounds Antarctica every winter. In fact, he sailed all the way around the continent but never saw it. Cook went farther south than anyone had ever gone. His record lasted 50 years.

Forty years after Cook, a new kind of seamen sailed the icy waters. They were hunters of seals and whales. Sailing through unknown waters in search of seals and whales, these men became explorers as well as hunters. The first person known to sight Antarctica was an American hunter, 21-year-old Nathaniel Brown Palmer in 1820.

Directions: Draw a ✓ in the box for the correct answer.

1. The main idea is:
   - ☐ Antarctica was not sighted until the early nineteenth century.
   - ☑ Many brave explorers and adventurers have sailed south to conquer the icy land.
2. The first person to sail to the ice field that surrounds Antarctica was:
   - ☐ Nathaniel Brown Palmer
   - ☑ Captain James Cook
   - ☐ Neal Armstrong
3. The first person known to sight Antarctica was:
   - ☐ an unknown ancient Greek
   - ☐ Captain James Cook
   - ☑ Nathaniel Brown Palmer
4. His profession was:
   - ☑ hunter
   - ☐ ship captain
   - ☐ explorer

65

Recognizing Details: The Frozen Continent

66

Directions: Read the information about explorers. Then, answer the questions.

By the mid-1800s, most of the seals of Antarctica had been killed. The seal hunters no longer sailed the icy waters. The next group of explorers who took an interest in Antarctica were scientists. Of these, the man who took the most daring chances and made the most amazing discoveries was British Captain James Clark Ross.

Ross first made a name for himself sailing to the north. In 1831, he discovered the North Magnetic Pole—one of two places on Earth toward which a compass needle points. In 1840, Ross set out to find the South Magnetic Pole. He made many marvelous discoveries, including the Ross Sea, a great open sea beyond the ice packs that stopped other explorers, and the Ross Ice Shelf, a great floating sheet of ice bigger than all of France!

The next man to make his mark exploring Antarctica was British explorer Robert Falcon Scott. Scott set out in 1902 to find the South Pole. He and his team suffered greatly, but they were able to make it a third of the way to the pole. Back in England, Scott was a great hero. In 1910, he again attempted to become the first man to reach the South Pole. But this time he had competition: an explorer from Norway, Roald Amundsen, was also leading a team to the South Pole.

It was a brutal race. Both teams faced many hardships, but they pressed on. Finally, on December 14, 1911, Amundsen became the first man to reach the South Pole. Scott arrived on January 17, 1912. He was bitterly disappointed at not being first. The trip back was even more horrible. None of the five men in the Scott expedition survived.

1. After the seal hunters, who were the next group of explorers interested in Antarctica?
   scientists
2. What great discovery did James Ross make before ever sailing to Antarctica?
   He discovered the North Magnetic Pole.
3. What were two other great discoveries made by James Ross?
   Ross Sea Ross Ice Shelf
4. Who was the first person to reach the South Pole?
   Roald Amundsen

66

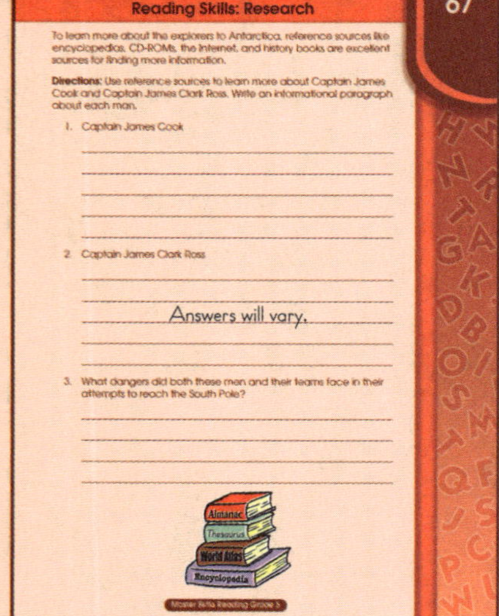

Reading Skills: Research

67

To learn more about the explorers to Antarctica, reference sources like encyclopedias, CD-ROMs, the Internet, and history books are excellent sources for finding more information.

Directions: Use reference sources to learn more about Captain James Cook and Captain James Clark Ross. Write an informational paragraph about each man.

1. Captain James Cook
2. Captain James Clark Ross

   Answers will vary.

3. What dangers did both these men and their teams face in their attempts to reach the South Pole?

67

Reading Comprehension: Polar Bears

68

Directions: Read the information about polar bears. Then, answer the questions by circling **Yes** or **No**.

Some animals are able to survive the cold weather and difficult conditions of the snow and ice fields in the Arctic polar regions. One of the best known is the polar bear.

Polar bears live on the land and the sea. They may drift hundreds of miles from land on huge sheets of floating ice. They use their great paws to paddle the ice along. Polar bears are excellent swimmers too. They can cross great distances of open water. While in the water, they feed mostly on fish and seals.

On land, these huge animals, which measure 10 feet long and weigh about 1,000 pounds, can run 25 miles an hour. Surprisingly, polar bears live as plant-eaters rather than hunters while on land. Unlike many kinds of bears, polar bears do not hibernate. They are active the whole year.

Baby polar bears are born during the winter. At birth, they are pink and almost hairless. These helpless cubs weigh only two pounds—less than one-third the size of most human infants. The mother bears raise their young in dens dug in snowbanks. By the time they are 10 weeks old, polar bear cubs are about the size of puppies and have enough white fur to protect them in the open air. The mothers give their cubs swimming, hunting, and fishing lessons. By the time autumn comes, the cubs are left to survive on their own.

1. Polar bears can live on the land and the sea. (Yes) No
2. Polar bears are excellent swimmers. (Yes) No
3. Polar bears hibernate in the winter. Yes (No)
4. A newborn polar bear weighs more than a newborn human baby. Yes (No)
5. Mother polar bears raise their babies in caves. Yes (No)
6. Father polar bears give the cubs swimming lessons. Yes (No)

68

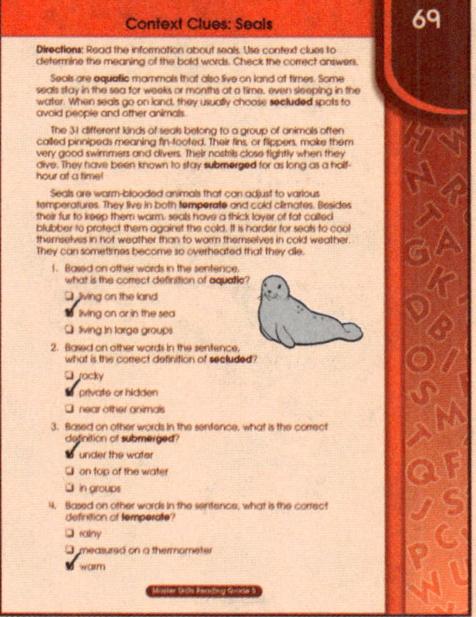

Context Clues: Seals

69

Directions: Read the information about seals. Use context clues to determine the meaning of the bold words. Check the correct answers.

Seals are **aquatic** mammals that also live on land at times. Some seals stay in the sea for weeks or months at a time, even sleeping in the water. When seals go on land, they usually choose **secluded** spots to avoid people and other animals.

The 31 different kinds of seals belong to a group of animals often called pinnipeds meaning fin-footed. Their fins, or flippers, make them very good swimmers and divers. Their nostrils close tightly when they dive. They have been known to stay **submerged** for as long as a half-hour at a time!

Seals are warm-blooded animals that can adjust to various temperatures. They live in both **temperate** and cold climates. Besides their fur to keep them warm, seals have a thick layer of fat called blubber to protect them against the cold. It is harder for seals to cool themselves in hot weather than to warm themselves in cold weather. They can sometimes become so overheated that they die.

1. Based on other words in the sentence, what is the correct definition of **aquatic**?
   - ☐ living on the land
   - ✔ living on or in the sea
   - ☐ living in large groups
2. Based on other words in the sentence, what is the correct definition of **secluded**?
   - ☐ rocky
   - ✔ private or hidden
   - ☐ near other animals
3. Based on other words in the sentence, what is the correct definition of **submerged**?
   - ✔ under the water
   - ☐ on top of the water
   - ☐ in groups
4. Based on other words in the sentence, what is the correct definition of **temperate**?
   - ☐ rainy
   - ☐ measured on a thermometer
   - ✔ warm

Master Skills Reading Grade 5

69

Reading Comprehension: Walruses

70

Directions: Read the information about walruses. Then, answer the questions.

A walrus is actually a type of seal that lives only in the Arctic Circle. It has two huge upper teeth, or tusks, which it uses to pull itself out of the water or to move over the rocks on land. It also uses its tusks to dig clams, one of its favorite foods, from the bottom of the sea. On an adult male walrus, the tusks may be three and a half feet long!

A walrus has an unusual face. Besides its long tusks, it has a big, bushy mustache made up of hundreds of movable, stiff bristles. These bristles also help the walrus push food into its mouth. Except for small wrinkles in the skin, a walrus has no outer ears.

Like a seal, the walrus uses its flippers to help it swim. Its front flippers serve as paddles, and while swimming, it swings the back of its huge body from side to side. A walrus looks awkward using its flippers to walk on land, but don't be fooled! A walrus can run as fast as a man.

Baby walruses are born in the early spring. They stay with their mothers until they are two years old. There is a good reason for this—they must grow little tusks, at least three or four inches long, before they can catch their own food from the bottom of the sea. Until then, they must stay close to their mothers to eat. A young walrus that is tired from swimming will climb onto its mother's back for a ride, holding onto her with its front flippers.

1. The walrus is a type of seal found only in the Arctic Circle
2. List two ways the walrus uses its tusks.
   to pull itself out of water — to dig clams
3. A walrus cannot move quickly on land. Yes (No) — **No**
4. A walrus has a large, bushy mustache. (Yes) No — **Yes**
5. A baby walrus stays very close to its mother until it is two years old. (Yes) No — **Yes**

Master Skills Reading Grade 5

70

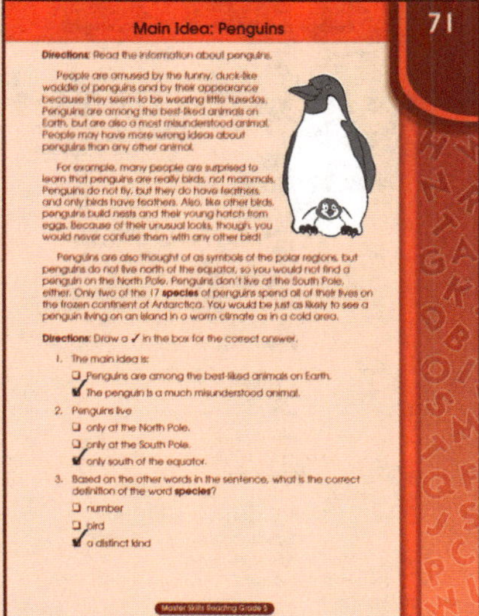

Main Idea: Penguins

71

Directions: Read the information about penguins.

People are amused by the funny, duck-like waddle of penguins and by their appearance because they seem to be wearing little tuxedos. Penguins are among the best-liked animals on Earth, but are also a most misunderstood animal. People may have more wrong ideas about penguins than any other animal.

For example, many people are surprised to learn that penguins are really birds, not mammals. Penguins do not fly, but they do have feathers, and only birds have feathers. Also, like other birds, penguins build nests and their young hatch from eggs. Because of their unusual looks, though, you would never confuse them with any other bird!

Penguins are also thought of as symbols of the polar regions, but penguins do not live north of the equator, so you would not find a penguin on the North Pole. Penguins don't live at the South Pole, either. Only two of the 17 **species** of penguins spend all of their lives on the frozen continent of Antarctica. You would be just as likely to see a penguin living on an island in a warm climate as in a cold area.

Directions: Draw a ✓ in the box for the correct answer.

1. The main idea is:
   - ☐ Penguins are among the best-liked animals on Earth.
   - ✔ The penguin is a much misunderstood animal.
2. Penguins live
   - ☐ only at the North Pole.
   - ☐ only at the South Pole.
   - ✔ only south of the equator.
3. Based on the other words in the sentence, what is the correct definition of the word **species**?
   - ☐ number
   - ☐ bird
   - ✔ a distinct kind

Master Skills Reading Grade 5

71

Review

72

Directions: Write a three-sentence summary for each of these selections. Refer to the reading selections for review if necessary.

1. "The Polar Trail"
2. "Polar Bears"
   Answers will vary.
3. "Walruses"

Directions: Write the main idea of these selections. Refer to the reading selections for review if necessary.

4. "The Frozen Continent"
   Beginning in the mid-1800s, a few brave scientists and explorers made many discoveries about Antarctica.
5. "Seals"
   Seals are mammals that have adapted to life in the sea and can live in various climates.

Master Skills Reading Grade 5

72

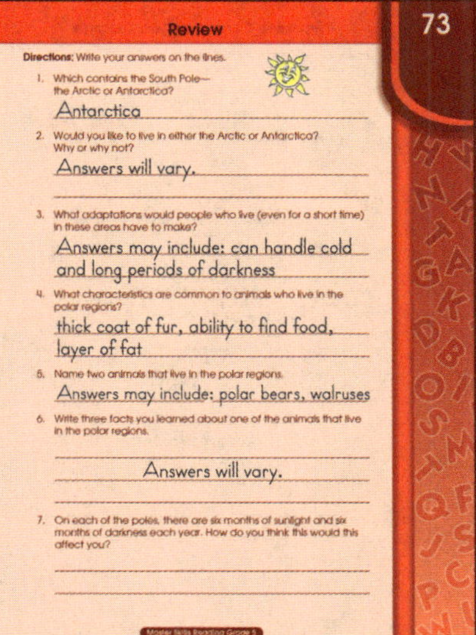

Review

73

Directions: Write your answers on the lines.

1. Which contains the South Pole—the Arctic or Antarctica?
   Antarctica
2. Would you like to live in either the Arctic or Antarctica? Why or why not?
   Answers will vary.
3. What adaptations would people who live (even for a short time) in these areas have to make?
   Answers may include: can handle cold and long periods of darkness
4. What characteristics are common to animals who live in the polar regions?
   thick coat of fur, ability to find food, layer of fat
5. Name two animals that live in the polar regions.
   Answers may include: polar bears, walruses
6. Write three facts you learned about one of the animals that live in the polar regions.
   Answers will vary.
7. On each of the poles, there are six months of sunlight and six months of darkness each year. How do you think this would this affect you?

Master Skills Reading Grade 5

73

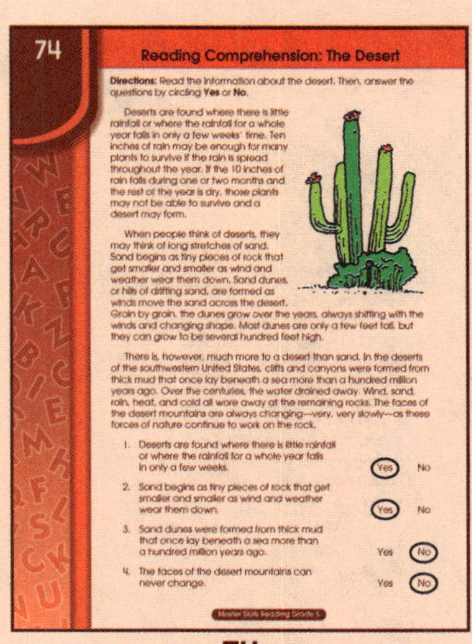

Reading Comprehension: The Desert

74

Directions: Read the information about the desert. Then, answer the questions by circling **Yes** or **No**.

Deserts are found where there is little rainfall or where the rainfall for a whole year falls in only a few weeks' time. Ten inches of rain may be enough for many plants to survive if the rain is spread throughout the year. If the 10 inches of rain falls during one or two months and the rest of the year is dry, those plants may not be able to survive and a desert may form.

When people think of deserts, they may think of long stretches of sand. Sand begins as tiny pieces of rock that get smaller and smaller as wind and weather wear them down. Sand dunes, or hills of drifting sand, are formed as winds move the sand across the desert. Grain by grain, the dunes grow over the years, always shifting with the winds and changing shape. Most dunes are only a few feet tall, but they can grow to be several hundred feet high.

There is, however, much more to a desert than sand. In the deserts of the southwestern United States, cliffs and canyons were formed from thick mud that once lay beneath a sea more than a hundred million years ago. Over the centuries, the water drained away. Wind, sand, rain, heat, and cold all wore away at the remaining rocks. The faces of the desert mountains are always changing—very, very slowly—as these forces of nature continue to work on the rock.

1. Deserts are found where there is little rainfall or where the rainfall for a whole year falls in only a few weeks. (Yes) No — **Yes**
2. Sand begins as tiny pieces of rock that get smaller and smaller as wind and weather wear them down. (Yes) No — **Yes**
3. Sand dunes were formed from thick mud that once lay beneath a sea more than a hundred million years ago. Yes (No) — **No**
4. The faces of the desert mountains can never change. Yes (No) — **No**

Master Skills Reading Grade 5

74

Answer Key

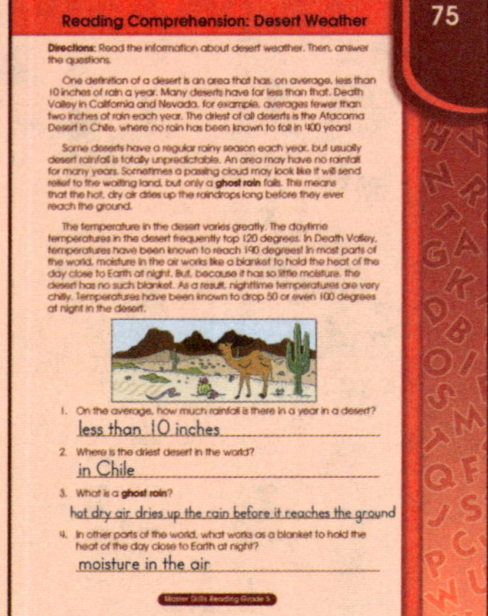

75

Reading Comprehension: Desert Weather

Directions: Read the information about desert weather. Then, answer the questions.

One definition of a desert is an area that has, on average, less than 10 inches of rain a year. Many deserts have far less than that. Death Valley in California and Nevada, for example, averages fewer than two inches of rain each year. The driest of all deserts is the Atacama Desert in Chile, where no rain has been known to fall in 400 years!

Some deserts have a regular rainy season each year, but usually desert rainfall is totally unpredictable. An area may have no rainfall for many years. Sometimes a passing cloud may look like it will send relief to the waiting land, but only a **ghost rain** falls. This means that the hot, dry air dries up the raindrops long before they ever reach the ground.

The temperature in the desert varies greatly. The daytime temperatures in the desert frequently top 120 degrees. In Death Valley, temperatures have been known to reach 190 degrees! In most parts of the world, moisture in the air works like a blanket to hold the heat of the day close to Earth at night. But, because it has so little moisture, the desert has no such blanket. As a result, nighttime temperatures are very chilly. Temperatures have been known to drop 50 or even 100 degrees at night in the desert.

1. On the average, how much rainfall is there in a year in a desert? less than 10 inches
2. Where is the driest desert in the world? in Chile
3. What is a **ghost rain**? hot dry air dries up the rain before it reaches the ground
4. In other parts of the world, what works as a blanket to hold the heat of the day close to Earth at night? moisture in the air

Master Skills Reading Grade 5

75

76

Review

Directions: Write a three-sentence summary of these selections which includes the main idea.

1. "The Desert"
2. "Desert Weather" Answers will vary.

Directions: Define these words. Then, use them in sentences of your own. Sample answers:

3. dunes hills of sand
4. canyon a deep valley with very steep sides
5. average usual, normal
6. unpredictable not known in advance

Master Skills Reading Grade 5

76

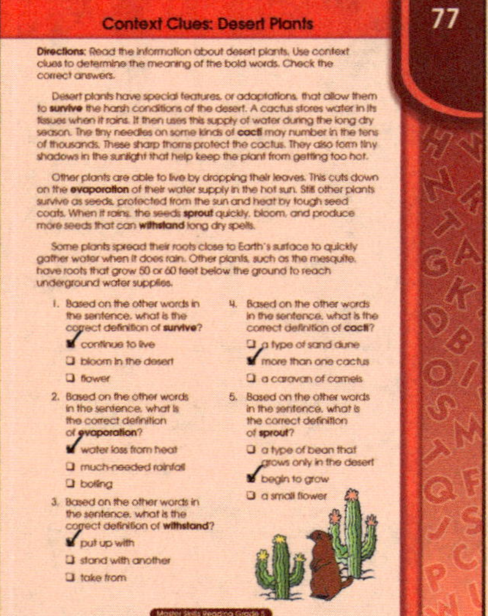

77

Context Clues: Desert Plants

Directions: Read the information about desert plants. Use context clues to determine the meaning of the bold words. Check the correct answers.

Desert plants have special features, or adaptations, that allow them to **survive** the harsh conditions of the desert. A cactus stores water in its tissues when it rains. It then uses this supply of water during the long dry season. The tiny needles on some kinds of **cacti** may number in the tens of thousands. These sharp thorns protect the cactus. They also form tiny shadows in the sunlight that help keep the plant from getting too hot.

Other plants are able to live by dropping their leaves. This cuts down on the **evaporation** of their water supply in the hot sun. Still other plants survive as seeds, protected from the sun and heat by tough seed coats. When it rains, the seeds **sprout** quickly, bloom, and produce more seeds that can **withstand** long dry spells.

Some plants spread their roots close to Earth's surface to quickly gather water when it does rain. Other plants, such as the mesquite, have roots that grow 50 or 60 feet below the ground to reach underground water supplies.

1. Based on the other words in the sentence, what is the correct definition of **survive**?
   - ✔ continue to live
   - ❑ bloom in the desert
   - ❑ flower
2. Based on the other words in the sentence, what is the correct definition of **evaporation**?
   - ✔ water loss from heat
   - ❑ much-needed rainfall
   - ❑ boiling
3. Based on the other words in the sentence, what is the correct definition of **withstand**?
   - ✔ put up with
   - ❑ stand with another
   - ❑ take from
4. Based on the other words in the sentence, what is the correct definition of **cacti**?
   - ❑ a type of sand dune
   - ✔ more than one cactus
   - ❑ a caravan of camels
5. Based on the other words in the sentence, what is the correct definition of **sprout**?
   - ❑ a type of bean that grows only in the desert
   - ✔ begin to grow
   - ❑ a small flower

Master Skills Reading Grade 5

77

78

Recognizing Details: The Cactus Family

Directions: Read the information about cacti. Pay close attention to details. Answer the questions.

Although cacti are the best-known desert plants, they don't live only in hot, dry places. While cacti are most likely to be found in the desert areas of Mexico and the southwestern United States, they can by seen as far north as Nova Scotia, Canada. Certain types of cactus can live even in the snow!

Desert cactus are particularly good at surviving very long dry spells. Most cacti have a very long root system so they can absorb as much water as possible. Every available drop of water is taken into the cactus and held in its fleshy stem. A cactus stem can hold enough water to last for two years or longer.

A cactus may be best known for its spines. Although a few kinds of cacti don't have spines, the stems of most types are covered with these sharp needles. The spines have many uses for a cactus. They keep animals from eating the cactus. They collect raindrops and dew. The spines also help keep the plant cool by forming shadows in the sun and by trapping a layer of air close to the plant. They break up the desert winds that dry out the cactus.

Cacti come in all sizes and shapes. The biggest type in North America is the saguaro. It can weigh 12,000 to 14,000 pounds and grow to be 50 feet tall. A saguaro can last several years without water, but it will grow only after summer rains. In May and June, white blossoms appear. Many kinds of birds nest in these enormous cacti: white-winged doves, woodpeckers, small owls, thrashers, and wrens all build nests in the saguaro.

1. Where are you most likely to find a cactus growing? in deserts
2. How long can most cacti survive without water? two years or longer
3. What are two ways the spines help a cactus? collect moisture from cooling shadows, keep animals from eating the plant
4. What animals live in a saguaro cactus? doves, woodpeckers, owls, thrashers, wrens

Master Skills Reading Grade 5

78

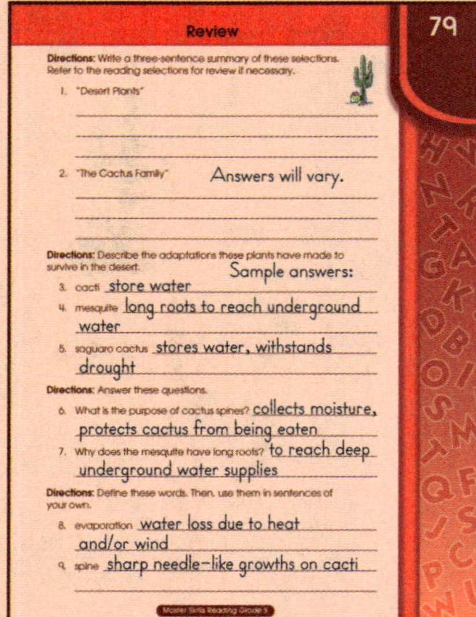

79

Review

Directions: Write a three-sentence summary of these selections. Refer to the reading selections for review if necessary.

1. "Desert Plants"
2. "The Cactus Family" Answers will vary.

Directions: Describe the adaptations these plants have made to survive in the desert. Sample answers:

3. cacti store water
4. mesquite long roots to reach underground water
5. saguaro cactus stores water, withstands drought

Directions: Answer these questions.

6. What is the purpose of cactus spines? collects moisture, protects cactus from being eaten
7. Why does the mesquite have long roots? to reach deep underground water supplies

Directions: Define these words. Then, use them in sentences of your own.

8. evaporation water loss due to heat and/or wind
9. spine sharp needle-like growths on cacti

Master Skills Reading Grade 5

79

80

Reading Comprehension: Lizards

Directions: Read the information about lizards. Then, answer the questions.

Lizards are reptiles, related to snakes, turtles, alligators, and crocodiles. Like other reptiles, lizards are cold-blooded. This means their body temperature changes with that of their surroundings. However, by changing their behavior throughout the day, they can keep their temperature fairly constant.

Lizards are among the many animals that live in deserts. They usually come out of their burrows early in the morning. Most lizards lie in the sun to get warm before starting their daily activities. In mid-morning, they hunt for food. If it becomes too hot, lizards can raise their tails and bodies off the ground to help cool off. At mid-day, they return to their burrows or crawl under rocks for several hours. Late in the day, they again lie in the sun to absorb heat before the chilly desert night falls.

Like all animals, lizards have ways of protecting themselves. Some types of lizards have developed a most unusual defense. If a hawk or other animal grabs one of these lizards by its tail, the tail will break off. The tail will continue to wiggle around to distract the attacker while the lizard runs away. A month or two later, the lizard grows a new tail.

There are about 3,000 kinds of lizards, and all of them can bite, but only two types of lizards are poisonous: the Gila monster of the southwestern United States and the Mexican bearded lizard. Both are short-legged, thick-bodied reptiles with fat tails. These lizards do not attack people and will not bite them unless they are attacked.

1. What can a lizard do if it becomes too hot? raise its tail and body off the ground, crawl in burrows or under rocks
2. What is an unusual defense some lizards have developed to protect themselves? tails will break off and distract predators
3. What two types of lizards are poisonous? Gila monster and Mexican bearded lizard

Master Skills Reading Grade 5

80

Answer Key

Main Idea: People in the Desert

81

Directions: Read the information about people in the desert. Then, answer the questions.

Long before Europeans came to live in America, Native Americans had discovered ways of living in the desert. Some of these Native Americans were hunters or belonged to wandering tribes that stayed in the desert for only short periods of time. Others learned to farm and live in villages. They made their houses of trees, clay, and brush.

The desert met all of their needs for life: food, water, skins for clothing, materials for tools, weapons, and shelter. For meat, the desert offered deer, birds, and rabbits for hunting. When these animals were hard to find, the Native Americans would eat mice and lizards. Many desert plants, such as the prickly pear and mesquite, provided moisture, fruit, and seeds that could be eaten.

The first Europeans in the American deserts were searching for furs and metals, like silver and gold. They explored, but did not settle in the desert. The early pioneers were usually unsuccessful at living in the desert. They found the great heat and long dry periods too difficult. When they moved away, they left behind empty mining camps, houses, and sheds that slowly fell apart in the sun and wind.

1. What is the main idea of this selection?
   - ☑ Before Europeans came to live in America, Native Americans had discovered ways of successfully living in the desert.
   - ☐ Some Native Americans were hunters or belonged to wandering tribes who stayed in the desert for only short periods of time.
2. Who were the first people to live in the deserts of North America?
   Native Americans
3. What kinds of food did the Native Americans find in the desert?
   meat, desert plants
4. What were the first Europeans who came to the desert looking for?
   furs and metals (silver and gold)

Master Skills Reading Grade 5

81

Main Idea: Camels

82

Directions: Read the information about camels. Then, answer the questions.

Camels are well suited to desert life. They can cope with infrequent supplies of food and water, blazing heat during the day, low temperatures at night, and sand blown by high winds.

There are two kinds of camels: the two-humped bactrian and the one-humped dromedary. The dromedary is the larger of the two. It has coarse fur on its back that helps protect it from the sun's rays. The hair on its stomach and legs is short to prevent overheating. When camels **molt** in the spring, their wool can be collected in tufts from the bushes and ground.

The legs of the dromedary are much longer than those of the bactrian. Animals that live in very hot countries tend to have longer legs. This gives them a larger area of body surface from which heat can escape. Bactrian camels live in the deserts of central Asia where winters are bitterly cold, so they are not as tall as dromedaries.

Both kinds of camels have pads on their feet that keep them from sinking into the sand as they walk. A camel's long neck allows it to reach the ground to drink water and eat grass without having to bend its legs. It also can reach up to eat leaves from trees.

Camels do not store water in their humps as many people believe. The hump is for fat storage. When there is plenty of food, the camel's hump swells and feels firm. During the dry season when there is little food, the fat is used up and the hump shrinks and becomes soft.

1. What is the main idea of this selection?
   - ☑ Camels are well suited to desert life.
   - ☐ There are two kinds of camels.
2. Based on the other words in the sentence, what is the correct definition of **molt**?
   - ☐ turns into a butterfly
   - ☑ sheds its hair
   - ☐ becomes overheated
3. What are the two kinds of camels?
   bactrian and dromedary
4. Why don't camels sink into the sand when they walk?
   They have pads on their feet.

Master Skills Reading Grade 5

82

Review

83

Directions: Write your answers in complete sentences.

1. Describe how the cold-blooded lizard regulates its body temperature.
   It lies in the sun to get warm in the morning. It raises its tail and body off the ground to cool off. It hides in burrows or under rocks to cool off. It lies in the sun late in the day to absorb warmth before night.
2. What is the main idea of the selection "Lizards"?
   Lizards have adapted to desert life in many ways.
3. Describe how Native Americans adapted to life in the desert.
   They made homes of available materials. They learned to find food, water, shelter, and clothing.
4. Why do you think early pioneers were unsuccessful at desert living?
   Answers will vary.
5. Describe the adaptations of camels for successful desert habitation.
   They store fat in their humps, cope with little food or water, have long legs for larger body surface, fur to protect from sun's rays, pads on feet, etc.

Master Skills Reading Grade 5

83

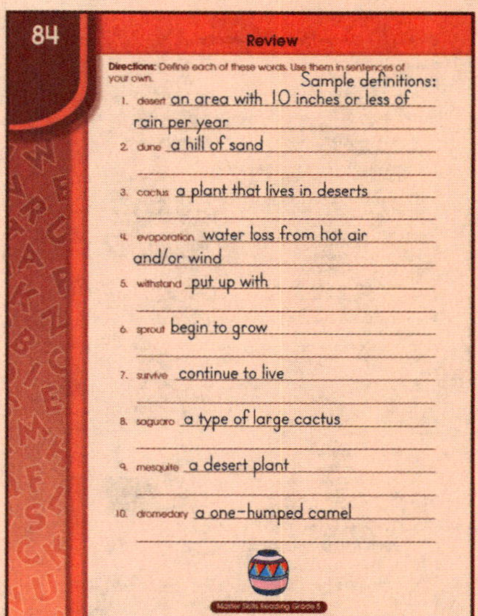

Review

84

Directions: Define each of these words. Use them in sentences of your own.

Sample definitions:

1. desert an area with 10 inches or less of rain per year
2. dune a hill of sand
3. cactus a plant that lives in deserts
4. evaporation water loss from hot air and/or wind
5. withstand put up with
6. sprout begin to grow
7. survive continue to live
8. saguaro a type of large cactus
9. mesquite a desert plant
10. dromedary a one-humped camel

Master Skills Reading Grade 5

84

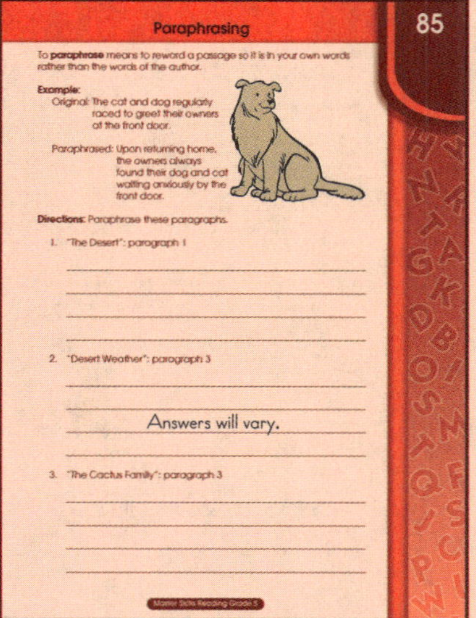

Paraphrasing

85

To **paraphrase** means to reword a passage so it is in your own words rather than the words of the author.

Example:

Original: The cat and dog regularly raced to greet their owners at the front door.

Paraphrased: Upon returning home, the owners always found their dog and cat waiting anxiously by the front door.

Directions: Paraphrase these paragraphs.

1. "The Desert": paragraph 1
2. "Desert Weather": paragraph 3
3. "The Cactus Family": paragraph 3

Answers will vary.

Master Skills Reading Grade 5

85

Reading Comprehension: Desert Lakes

86

Directions: Read the information about lakes in the desert. Then, answer the questions.

A few deserts have small permanent lakes. While they may be a welcome sight in the desert, the water in them is not fit for drinking. They are salt lakes. Rain from nearby higher land keeps these lakes supplied with water, but the lakes are blocked in with nowhere to drain. Over the years, mineral salts collect in the water and build up to a high level, making the water undrinkable.

Most desert lakes are only temporary. Occasional rains may fill them to depths of several feet, but in a matter of weeks or months, all the water has been dried up by the heat and sun. The dried lake beds that remain are called **playas**. Some playas are simply areas of sun-baked mud; others are covered with a sparkling layer of salt.

Perhaps the most unusual desert lake is in central Australia. It is called Lake Eyre. It is a huge lake—nearly 3,600 square miles in area—but it is almost totally dry most of the time. Since it was discovered in 1840, it has been filled only two times. Both times, the lake completely dried up again within a few years.

1. Why is the water in a desert lake not fit for drinking?
   It is salt water.
2. Why are the lakes in the desert salt lakes?
   Mineral salts collect there.
3. Why are most desert lakes only temporary?
   The water evaporates.
4. What is a **playa**? a dried lake bed
5. What is the name of the unusual desert lake in central Australia?
   Lake Eyre

Master Skills Reading Grade 5

86

Answer Key

87 — Review

Directions: Write your answers in complete sentences.

1. What is a desert?
   A desert is an area where less than 10 inches of rain falls per year.
2. Name a desert in the United States and tell where it is.
   Answers will vary.
3. What special characteristics must an animal have to survive in the desert?
   It must be able to tolerate extremes of heat and cold, be able to protect itself from the sun's rays, and be able to find or store food and water.
4. What special characteristics must a plant have to survive in the desert?
   It must have a way to collect or store moisture, withstand long dry periods, and tolerate extremes of heat and cold.
5. Would you like to visit the desert? Why or why not?
   Answers will vary.

Master Skills Reading Grade 5

87

88 — Reading Comprehension: Railroads

Directions: Read the information about railroads. Then, answer the questions.

As early as the 1550s, a rough form of railroad was already being used in parts of Europe. Miners in England and other areas of western Europe used horse- or mule-drawn wagons on wooden tracks to pull loads out of mines. With these tracks, the horses could pull twice as much weight as they could without them. No one could have known then that one day this simple idea would change the world.

There were many developments along the way that helped make railroads a practical and valuable form of transportation. Two of the most important were the iron track and the "flanged" wheel, which has a rim around it to hold it onto the track. The most important invention was the steam engine by James Watt in 1765.

The first railroads in the United States were built during the late 1820s and caused a lot of excitement. They were faster than other forms of travel, and they could provide service year-round, unlike boats and stagecoaches. Trains were soon the main means of travel in the U.S.

Railroads played a major part in the Industrial Revolution—the years of change when machines were first used to do work that had been done by hand for many centuries. Trains provided cheaper rates and quicker service for transporting goods. Because manufacturers could ship their goods over long distances, they could sell their products all over the nation instead of only in the surrounding cities and towns. This meant greater profits for the companies. Trains also brought people into the cities to work in factories.

1. What was the source of power for the earliest railroads?
   horses or mules
2. What were three important developments that made railroads a practical means of transportation?
   iron track
   "flanged" wheels
   steam engine
3. What is meant by the Industrial Revolution? the years of change from people-made to machine-made products

Master Skills Reading Grade 5

88

89 — Main Idea: Locomotives

Directions: Read the information about locomotives. Then, answer the questions.

In the 1800s, the steam locomotive was considered by many to be a symbol of the new Industrial Age. It was, indeed, one of the most important inventions of the time. Over the years, there have been many changes to the locomotive. One of the most important has been its source of power. During its history, the locomotive has gone from steam to electric to diesel power.

The first railroads used horses or mules for power, but the development of the steam locomotive made railroads a practical means of transportation. The first steam locomotive was built in 1804 in Great Britain by Richard Trevithick. It could haul 50,000 pounds, but it was not very successful because it was so heavy it caused the tracks to fall apart. However, it encouraged other engineers to try to build steam locomotives. Two of the most important men to accept the challenge were George Stephenson and his son, Robert. Robert once won a contest to build the best locomotive. *The Rocket*, as he called it, had a top speed of 29 miles per hour.

In America, developments in steam engines were close behind those of the British. In 1830, Peter Cooper's tiny locomotive, called *Tom Thumb*, lost a famous race against a horse-drawn coach. In spite of the loss, it still convinced railroad officials that steam power was more practical than horsepower.

Just before the turn of the century, the electric locomotive was widely used. At its peak in the 1940s, U.S. railroads had 2,400 miles of electric routes.

The diesel locomotive was invented in the 1890s by Rudolf Diesel, a German engineer. The power of this locomotive was supplied by a diesel fuel engine. The diesel locomotive is still used today. It costs about twice as much as a steam locomotive to build, but it is much cheaper to operate.

1. What is the main idea of this selection?
   - ☐ The steam locomotive was considered a symbol of the Industrial Age.
   - ☑ Over the years, there have been many changes to the locomotive.
2. Who built the first steam locomotive in 1804?
   Richard Trevithick
3. How fast could *The Rocket* travel?
   29 miles per hour

Master Skills Reading Grade 5

89

90 — Review

Directions: Define these words as used in the selections "Railroads" and "Locomotives."

1. flanged wheel: wheel which has a rim around it to hold it to a track
2. transportation: a way to move people and products from one place to another
3. profit: money earned
4. locomotive: a vehicle that pulls a train
5. diesel: a type of fuel
6. engineer: a person who drives a train

Directions: Write your answer in a complete sentence.

7. The world is going through another "revolution" in industry today. What new technology is leading this change and how might it affect workers in the future?
   Answers will vary.

Master Skills Reading Grade 5

90

91 — Reading Comprehension: Railroad Pioneer

Directions: Read the information about railroad pioneers. Then, answer the questions by circling **Yes** or **No**.

George Stephenson was born in Wylam, England, in 1781. His family was extremely poor. When he was young, he didn't go to school but worked in the coal mines. In his spare time, he taught himself to read and write. After a series of explosions in the coal pits, Stephenson built a miner's safety lamp. This helped bring him to the attention of the owners of the coal mines. They put him in charge of all the machinery.

In 1812, Stephenson became an engine builder for the mines. The owners were interested in locomotives because the cost of horse feed was so high. They wanted Stephenson to build a locomotive to pull the coal cars from the mines. His first locomotive, *The Blucher*, was put on the rails in 1814.

Stephenson was a good engineer, and he was fortunate to work for a rich employer. Between 1814 and 1826, Stephenson was the only man in Great Britain building locomotives.

When the Stockholm and Darlington Railway, the first public railroad system, was planned, Stephenson was named company engineer. He convinced the owners to use steam power instead of horses. He built the first locomotive on the line. *The Locomotion*, as it was called, was the best locomotive that had been built anywhere in the world up to that time. Over the years, Stephenson was responsible for many other important developments in locomotive design, such as improved cast-iron rails and wheels, and the first steel springs strong enough to carry several tons.

Stephenson was convinced that the future of railroads lay in steam power. His great vision of what the railroad system could become was a driving force in the early years of its development.

1. George Stephenson was an excellent student in school. Yes **(No)**
2. Stephenson's first invention was a miner's safety lamp. **(Yes)** No
3. Between 1814 and 1826, Stephenson was one of many engineers building locomotives in Great Britain. Yes **(No)**
4. The Stockholm and Darlington Railway was the first public railroad system. **(Yes)** No
5. The first locomotive on the Stockholm and Darlington line was *The Locomotion*, built by Stephenson. **(Yes)** No

Master Skills Reading Grade 5

91

92 — Tall Tales

A **tall tale** is a fictional story with exaggerated details and a "super" hero. The main character in a tall tale is much larger, stronger, smarter, or better than a real person. Tall tales may be unbelievable, but they are fun to hear.

Directions: Read the story about John Henry. Then, answer the questions.

A Steel-Driving Man

On the night John Henry was born, forked lightning split the air and the earth shook. He weighed 44 pounds at birth, and the first thing he did was reach for a hammer hanging on the wall. "He's going to be a steel-driving man," his father told his mother.

One night, John Henry dreamed he was working on a railroad. Every time his hammer hit a spike, the sky lit up with the sparks. "I dreamed that the railroad was going to be the end of me, and I'd die with a hammer in my hand," he said. When John Henry grew up he did work for the railroad. He was the fastest, most powerful steel-driving man in the world.

In about 1870, the steam drill was invented. One day the company at the far end of a tunnel tried it out. John Henry's company, working at the other end, continued to use men to do the drilling. There was much bragging from both companies as to which was faster. Finally, they decided to have a contest. John Henry was matched against the best man with a steam drill.

John Henry swung a 20-pound hammer in each hand. The sparks flew so fast and hot that they burned his face. At the end of the day, the judges said John Henry had beaten the steam drill by four feet!

That night, John Henry said, "I was a steel-driving man." Then, he laid down and closed his eyes forever.

1. How much was John Henry said to have weighed at birth?
   44 pounds
2. Why did his father think he would be a steel-driving man?
   He reached for a hammer first.
3. What invention was John Henry in a contest against? steam drill
4. Who won the contest? John Henry
5. What happened to John Henry after the contest? He died.

Master Skills Reading Grade 5

92

Tall Tales

Directions: Write a tall tale about yourself. Be sure to make it a fantastic and incredible story!

Answers will vary.

Directions: Reread your tall tale. Does it make sense? Check and correct spelling and grammar mistakes. Does your story fit the category of a tall tale?

93

Context Clues: Passenger Cars

Directions: Read the information about passenger cars. Use context clues to determine the meaning of words in bold. Check the correct answers.

Early railroad passenger cars were little more than stagecoaches fitted with special wheels to help them stay on the tracks. They didn't hold many passengers, and because they were made out of wood, they were fire hazards. They also did not hold up very well if the train came off the track or had a **collision** with another train.

In the United States, it wasn't long before passenger cars were lengthened to hold more people. Late in the 1830s, Americans were riding in **elongated** cars with double seats on either side of a center aisle. By the early 1900s, most cars were made of metal instead of wood.

Sleeping and dining cars were introduced in the United States by the early 1860s. Over the next 25 years other improvements were made, including electric lighting, steam heat, and covered **vestibules** that allowed passengers to walk between cars. All of these **luxuries** helped make railroad travel much more comfortable.

1. Based on the other words in the sentence, what is the correct definition of **collision**?
   - ✔ crash
   - ❑ race
   - ❑ track
2. Based on the other words in the sentence, what is the correct definition of **elongated**?
   - ❑ wooden
   - ❑ new
   - ✔ lengthened
3. Based on the other words in the sentence, what is the correct definition of **vestibules**?
   - ✔ passageways
   - ❑ cars
   - ❑ depots
4. Based on the other words in the sentence, what is the correct definition of **luxuries**?
   - ❑ additions
   - ✔ things offering the greatest comfort
   - ❑ inventions

94

Reading Skills: Railroads

Directions: Read the information about railroads. Then, answer the questions.

When railroads became the major means of transportation, they replaced earlier forms of travel, like the stagecoach. Railroads remained the unchallenged leader for a hundred years. Beginning in the early 1900s, railroads faced **competition** from newer forms of transportation.

Today, millions of people have their own automobiles. Buses offer inexpensive travel between cities. Large trucks haul goods across the country. Airplanes provide quick transportation over long distances. The result has been a sharp drop in the use of trains.

Today, nearly all railroads face serious problems that threaten to drive them out of business. But railroads still provide low-cost, fuel-saving transportation that will remain important. One gallon of diesel fuel will haul about four times as much by railroad as by truck. In a time when the world is concerned about saving fuel, this is one area in which the railroads still have much to offer.

1. What is the main idea of this selection?
   - ❑ When railroads became the major means of transportation, they replaced earlier forms of travel.
   - ✔ Beginning in the early 1900s, railroads have faced competition from newer forms of transportation.
2. Based on the other words in the sentence, what is the correct definition of **competition**?
   - ✔ businesses trying to get the same customers
   - ❑ problems
   - ❑ support
3. What are four newer forms of transportation that have challenged railroads?

   cars, trucks, buses, airplanes

95

Review

Directions: Write your answers in complete sentences.

1. Today, we have machines which are capable of putting in railroad tracks. However, in the 1800s, all the work was done by hand. What dangers and difficulties might railroad workers have faced?

   Answers will vary.

2. Why was the railroad a major contributor to the Industrial Revolution?

   Answers may include: Faster, better transportation increased the demand for more products, which could be sold far from where they were made.

3. Compare traveling by train to traveling by one other form of transportation, past or present. Discuss the advantages and disadvantages of both.

   Answers will vary.

96

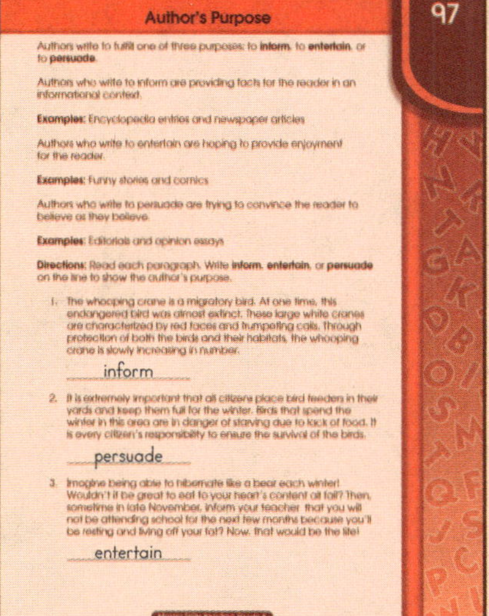

Author's Purpose

Authors write to fulfill one of three purposes: to **inform**, to **entertain**, or to **persuade**.

Authors who write to inform are providing facts for the reader in an informational context.

Examples: Encyclopedia entries and newspaper articles

Authors who write to entertain are hoping to provide enjoyment for the reader.

Examples: Funny stories and comics

Authors who write to persuade are trying to convince the reader to believe as they believe.

Examples: Editorials and opinion essays

Directions: Read each paragraph. Write **inform**, **entertain**, or **persuade** on the line to show the author's purpose.

1. The whooping crane is a migratory bird. At one time, this endangered bird was almost extinct. These large white cranes are characterized by red faces and trumpeting calls. Through protection of both the birds and their habitats, the whooping crane is slowly increasing in number.

   inform

2. It is extremely important that all citizens place bird feeders in their yards and keep them full for the winter. Birds that spend the winter in this area are in danger of starving due to lack of food. It is every citizen's responsibility to ensure the survival of the birds.

   persuade

3. Imagine being able to hibernate like a bear each winter! Wouldn't it be great to eat to your heart's content all fall? Then, sometime in late November, inform your teacher that you will not be attending school for the next few months because you'll be resting and living off your fat? Now, that would be the life!

   entertain

97

Author's Purpose

Directions: Write a paragraph of your own for each purpose. The paragraph can be about any topic.

1. to inform
2. to persuade

   Answers will vary.

3. to entertain

98

Answer Key

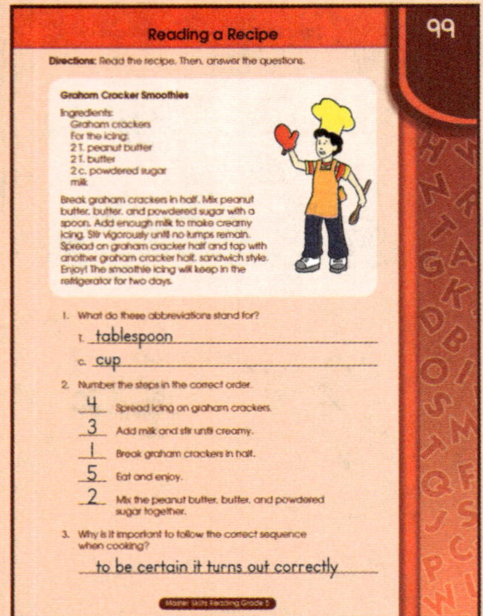

Reading a Recipe

Directions: Read the recipe. Then, answer the questions.

Graham Cracker Smoothies

Ingredients:
Graham crackers
For the icing:
2 T. peanut butter
2 T. butter
2 c. powdered sugar
milk

Break graham crackers in half. Mix peanut butter, butter, and powdered sugar with a spoon. Add enough milk to make creamy icing. Stir vigorously until no lumps remain. Spread on graham cracker half and top with another graham cracker half, sandwich style. Enjoy! The smoothie icing will keep in the refrigerator for two days.

1. What do these abbreviations stand for?
   T. tablespoon
   c. cup
2. Number the steps in the correct order.
   4 Spread icing on graham crackers.
   3 Add milk and stir until creamy.
   1 Break graham crackers in half.
   5 Eat and enjoy.
   2 Mix the peanut butter, butter, and powdered sugar together.
3. Why is it important to follow the correct sequence when cooking?
   to be certain it turns out correctly

99

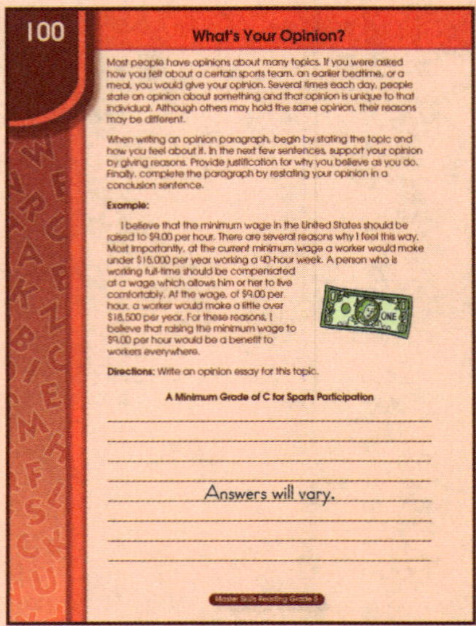

What's Your Opinion?

Most people have opinions about many topics. If you were asked how you felt about a certain sports team, an earlier bedtime, or a meal, you would give your opinion. Several times each day, people state an opinion about something and that opinion is unique to that individual. Although others may hold the same opinion, their reasons may be different.

When writing an opinion paragraph, begin by stating the topic and how you feel about it. In the next few sentences, support your opinion by giving reasons. Provide justification for why you believe as you do. Finally, complete the paragraph by restating your opinion in a conclusion sentence.

Example:

I believe that the minimum wage in the United States should be raised to $9.00 per hour. There are several reasons why I feel this way. Most importantly, at the current minimum wage a worker would make under $15,000 per year working a 40-hour week. A person who is working full-time should be compensated at a wage which allows him or her to live comfortably. At the wage, of $9.00 per hour, a worker would make a little over $18,500 per year. For these reasons, I believe that raising the minimum wage to $9.00 per hour would be a benefit to workers everywhere.

Directions: Write an opinion essay for this topic.

A Minimum Grade of C for Sports Participation

Answers will vary.

100

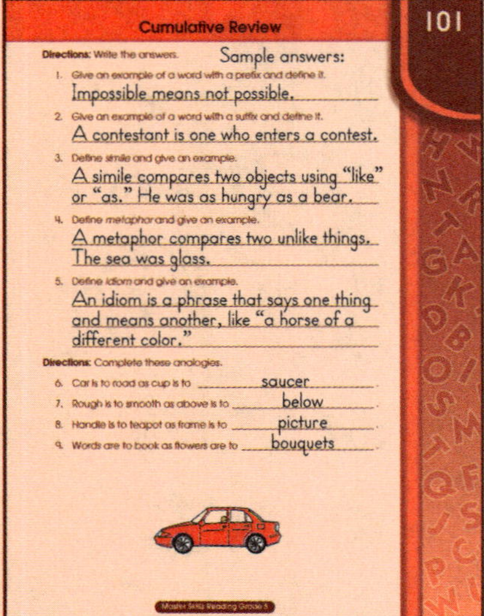

Cumulative Review

Directions: Write the answers. Sample answers:

1. Give an example of a word with a prefix and define it.
   Impossible means not possible.
2. Give an example of a word with a suffix and define it.
   A contestant is one who enters a contest.
3. Define *simile* and give an example.
   A simile compares two objects using "like" or "as." He was as hungry as a bear.
4. Define *metaphor* and give an example.
   A metaphor compares two unlike things. The sea was glass.
5. Define *idiom* and give an example.
   An idiom is a phrase that says one thing and means another, like "a horse of a different color."

Directions: Complete these analogies.

6. Car is to road as cup is to saucer.
7. Rough is to smooth as above is to below.
8. Handle is to teapot as frame is to picture.
9. Words are to book as flowers are to bouquets.

101

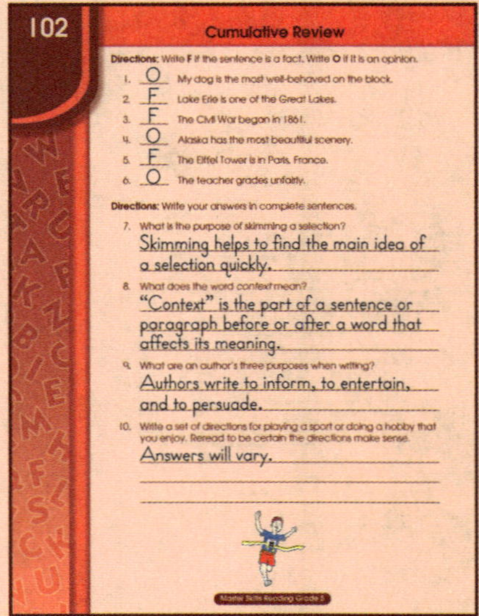

Cumulative Review

Directions: Write **F** if the sentence is a fact. Write **O** if it is an opinion.

1. O My dog is the most well-behaved on the block.
2. F Lake Erie is one of the Great Lakes.
3. F The Civil War began in 1861.
4. O Alaska has the most beautiful scenery.
5. F The Eiffel Tower is in Paris, France.
6. O The teacher grades unfairly.

Directions: Write your answers in complete sentences.

7. What is the purpose of skimming a selection?
   Skimming helps to find the main idea of a selection quickly.
8. What does the word *context* mean?
   "Context" is the part of a sentence or paragraph before or after a word that affects its meaning.
9. What are an author's three purposes when writing?
   Authors write to inform, to entertain, and to persuade.
10. Write a set of directions for playing a sport or doing a hobby that you enjoy. Reread to be certain the directions make sense.
    Answers will vary.

102

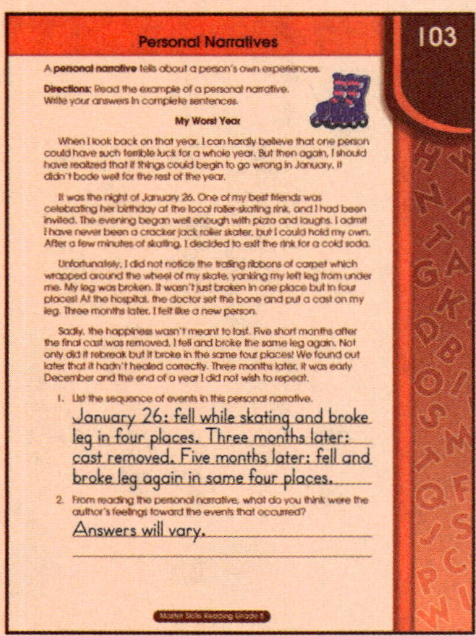

Personal Narratives

A **personal narrative** tells about a person's own experiences.

Directions: Read the example of a personal narrative. Write your answers in complete sentences.

My Worst Year

When I look back on that year, I can hardly believe that one person could have such terrible luck for a whole year. But then again, I should have realized that if things could begin to go wrong in January, it didn't bode well for the rest of the year.

It was the night of January 26. One of my best friends was celebrating her birthday at the local roller-skating rink, and I had been invited. The evening began well enough with pizza and laughs. I admit I have never been a cracker jack roller skater, but I could hold my own. After a few minutes of skating, I decided to exit the rink for a cold soda.

Unfortunately, I did not notice the trailing ribbons of carpet which wrapped around the wheel of my skate, yanking my left leg from under me. My leg was broken. It wasn't just broken in one place but in four places! At the hospital, the doctor set the bone and put a cast on my leg. Three months later, I felt like a new person.

Sadly, the happiness wasn't meant to last. Five short months after the final cast was removed, I fell and broke the same leg again. Not only did it rebreak but it broke in the same four places! We found out later that it hadn't healed correctly. Three months later, it was early December and the end of a year I did not wish to repeat.

1. List the sequence of events in this personal narrative.
   January 26: fell while skating and broke leg in four places. Three months later: cast removed. Five months later: fell and broke leg again in same four places.
2. From reading the personal narrative, what do you think were the author's feelings toward the events that occurred?
   Answers will vary.

103

Personal Narratives

Directions: Using the personal narrative on the previous page as an example, write a narrative about an experience of your own. When you finish, remember to reread your narrative. Check for and correct spelling, grammar, and punctuation mistakes.

Answers will vary.

104

Complete the Story

Directions: Read the beginning of this story. Then, complete the story with your own ideas.

It was a beautiful summer day in June when my family and I set off on vacation. We were headed for Portsmouth, New Hampshire. There, we planned to go on a whale-watching ship and perhaps spy a humpback whale or two. However, there were many miles between our home and Portsmouth.

We camped at many lovely parks along the way to New Hampshire. We stayed in the Adirondack Mountains for a few days and then visited the White Mountains of Vermont before crossing into New Hampshire.

My family enjoys tent camping. My dad says you can't really get a taste of the great outdoors in a pop-up camper or RV. I love sitting by the fire at night, gazing at the stars, and listening to the animal noises.

The trip was going well, and everyone was enjoying our vacation. We made it to Portsmouth and were looking forward to the whale-watching adventure. We arrived at the dock a few minutes early. The ocean looked rough, but we had taken seasickness medication. We thought we were prepared for any kind of weather.

Answers will vary.

105

Newspapers as Learning Tools

Newspapers are one of the most convenient and versatile learning tools you have around your house. Encourage your child to read parts of the newspaper every day. You can help by asking your child to check some information for you. Questions like these will encourage your child to read the newspaper: "Will you check tomorrow's forecast?" or "Can you find out what's on TV at 7 tonight?" or "Who won the baseball game last night?"

You might notice a headline that looks interesting and ask your child to read the article and tell you what it is about. This will help him or her find the main idea of the article.

Look for articles of interest to your child—ones about neighborhood events, people you know, items relating to school or special hobbies, or sports of interest to your child. Sometimes, it helps to cut out the article and let your child read one article a day. It can be less intimidating to start by reading one short article than to try to read an entire newspaper.

Leave your newspaper folded in such a way that an interesting photo or headline is showing. That may help catch your child's attention and encourage him or her to read that article and others.

When an interesting story is developing in your local newspaper, encourage your child to follow it for several days to learn the latest developments.

Do you or your child have strong opinions about a local event, election, or proposed project? Encourage your child to read editorials by others with opposing viewpoints and to write an editorial to the paper expressing his or her views.

Tall Tales

Tall tales are fun to listen to and to tell. As you are traveling in the car, telling stories helps the time pass quickly. Look around for ideas to begin a tall tale—you'll find ideas on billboards and building signs or by listening to ads or songs on the radio.

Does a restaurant that specializes in chicken have a "Super Chicken" mascot? Ask your child, "What if Super Chicken came to life?" Make up stories together. Add exaggerated details. See who can make up the most outrageous adventures of Super Chicken, Manny the Marvelous Mechanic who can fix anything, or another made-up super hero.

Context Clues

As your child comes across words he or she doesn't know, help him or her use context clues to discover the meaning of new words. Encourage your child to use a dictionary to check or look for other meanings for that word.

Fact or Opinion?

Many ads are confusing or misleading. A child needs to be aware that not everything in an ad may be factual. Much of the appeal of ads is opinion. Cut ads from magazines and newspapers and listen to ads on television. Help your child sort through the information. Ask him or her to point out the parts that are facts and those that are opinions.

By realizing the difference and separating the two, your child will be able to make better judgments about which products to buy.

Reading Labels

Reading and understanding labels is a skill everyone needs. As you shop, let your child read labels to compare ingredients and other nutritional information. This will help your child become a better consumer and learn to eat more healthful foods.

Stress the importance of reading labels and following directions, particularly on medications or products that may be hazardous.

Following a Recipe

Let your child help with the cooking and baking. Not only does this give your child good experience in reading and following directions, but he or she will also use many math skills to measure ingredients. Have your child look for recipes in newspapers and magazines, as well as cookbooks. Most libraries have a large selection of cookbooks. It's a fun way to learn, and the results can be delicious.

If your child has made up a new recipe, encourage him or her to write it down and share it with others.

Homophone Challenge

Homophones are words that are pronounced the same but are spelled differently and have different meanings, like **to**, **two**, and **too**. Challenge your child to a contest to see who can write the most homophones.